PRACTICAL SOCIAL WORK

Series Editor: Jo Campling

> BASW

Social work is at an important stage in its development. All professions must be responsive to changing social and economic conditions if they are to meet the needs of those they serve. This series focuses on sound practice and the specific contribution which social workers can make to the well-being of our society.

The British Association of Social Workers has always been conscious of its role in setting guidelines for practice and in seeking to raise professional standards. The conception of the Practical Social Work series arose from a survey of BASW members to discover where they, the practitioners in social work, felt there was the most need for new literature. The response was overwhelming and enthusiastic, and the result is a carefully planned, coherent series of books. The emphasis is firmly on practice, set in a theoretical framework. The books will inform, stimulate and promote discussion, thus adding to the further development of skills and high professional standards. All the authors are practitioners and teachers of social work representing a wide variety of experience.

) CAMPLING

tles in this series follows overleaf

PRACTICAL SOCIAL WORK

Robert Adams *Social Work and Empowerment*

David Anderson *Social Work and Mental Handicap*

Sarah Banks *Ethics and Values in Social Work*

James G. Barber *Beyond Casework*

James G. Barber *Social Work with Addictions*

Peter Beresford and Suzy Croft *Citizen Involvement*

Suzy Braye and Michael Preston-Shoot *Practising Social Work Law* (2nd edn)

Robert Brown, Stanley Bute and Peter Ford *Social Workers at Risk*

Helen Cosis Brown *Social Work and Sexuality*

Alan Butler and Colin Pritchard *Social Workers and Mental Illness*

Crescy Cannan, Lynne Berry and Karen Lyons *Social Work and Europe*

Roger Clough *Residential Work*

David M. Cooper and David Ball *Social Work and Child Abuse*

Veronica Coulshed *Management in Social Work*

Veronica Coulshed and Joan Orme *Social Work Practice: An Introduction* (3rd edn)

Paul Daniel and John Wheeler *Social Work and Local Politics*

Peter R. Day *Sociology in Social Work Practice*

Lena Dominelli *Anti-Racist Social Work* (2nd edn)

Celia Doyle *Working with Abused Children*

Angela Everitt and Pauline Hardiker *Evaluating for Good Practice*

Angela Everitt, Pauline Hardiker, Jane Littlewood and audrey Mullender *Applied Research for Better Practice*

Kathy Ford and Alan Jones *Student Supervision*

David Francis and Paul Henderson *Working with Rural Communities*

Michael D.A. Freeman *Children, their Families and the Law*

Alison Froggatt *Family Work with Elderly People*

Danya Glaser and Stephen Frosh *Child Sexual Abuse* (2nd edn)

Bryan Glastonbury *Computers in Social Work*

Gill Gorell Barnes *Working with Families*

Cordelia Grimwood and Ruth Popplestone *Women, Management and Care*

Jalna Hanmer and Daphne Statham *Women and Social Work* (2nd edn)

Tony Jeffs and Mark Smith (eds) *Youth Work*

Michael Kerfoot and Alan Butler *Problems of Childhood and Adolescence*

Joyce Lishman *Communication in Social Work*

Carol Lupton and Terry Gillespie (eds) *Working with Violence*

Mary Marshall and Mary Dixon *Social Work with Older People* (3rd edn)

Paula Nicolson and Rowan Bayne *Applied Psychology for Social Workers* (2nd edn)

Kieran O'Hagan *Crisis Intervention in Social Services*

Michael Oliver and Bob Sapey *Social Work with Disabled People* (2nd edn)

Joan Orme and Bryan Glastonbury *Care Management*

Malcolm Payne *Social Care in the Community*

Malcolm Payne *Working in Teams*

John Pitts *Working with Young Offenders*

Michael Preston-Shoot *Effective Groupwork*

Peter Raynor, David Smith and Maurice Vanstone *Effective Probation Practice*

Steven Shardlow and Mark Doel *Practice Learning and Teaching*

Carole R. Smith *Social Work with the Dying and Bereaved*

Carole R. Smith, Mary T. Lane and Terry Walsh *Child Care and the Courts*

David Smith *Criminology for Social Work*

Gill Stewart and John Stewart *Social Work and Housing*

Christine Stones *Focus on Families*

Neil Thompson *Anti-Discriminatory Practice* (2nd edn)

Neil Thompson, Michael Murphy and Steve Stradling *Dealing with Stress*

Derek Tilbury *Working with Mental Illness*

Alan Twelvetrees *Community Work* (2nd edn)

Hilary Walker and Bill Beaumont (eds) *Working with Offenders*

Women and Social Work

Towards a woman-centred practice

Second edition

Jalna Hanmer and Daphne Statham

MACMILLAN

First published 1999 by
MACMILLAN PRESS LTD
Houndmills, Basingstoke, Hampshire RG21 6XS
and London
Companies and representatives
throughout the world

ISBN 0–333–69963–7 paperback

A catalogue record for this book is available
from the British Library.

This book is printed on paper suitable for recycling and
made from fully managed and sustained forest sources.

10 9 8 7 6 5 4 3 2 1
08 07 06 05 04 03 02 01 00 99

Editing and origination by
Aardvark Editorial, Mendham, Suffolk

Printed in Malaysia

Dedication

Each generation of women has the task of reconfirming, if not re-establishing, the individual and social worth of women. We dedicate this book to the current and the next generation of sisters in recognition of their efforts and potential to achieve a better future for women, one that recognises and values those who generate and maintain life.

Contents

Acknowledgements

The first edition of *Women and Social Work* acknowledged over 100 women who attended the Social Services Needs of Women courses, and we would like to do this again. Without them, the first edition would never have been written, nor the second. The concept of women-centred practice began with the courses held between 1983 and 1985, and developed through the participation of women in social and probation work.

We also wish to acknowledge the readers of the first edition for their contribution to raising the profile and increasing an understanding in social and care work of the central relevance of women in maintaining family and community life. This is part of the changed social context basic to the largely rewritten second edition.

With this second edition, we also would like to thank the many women who contributed to its completion: Charlee Brewsher, Audrey McCloud, Simone Standeven and Pam Todd who typed various drafts and prepared the text for publication, and Catherine Euler who helped in the completion of the bibliography. And finally, we wish to thank Jo Campling for ensuring, through her insistence and persistence, that we completed this overdue manuscript, and also Catherine Gray for her tolerance and patience.

1

Introduction to the Second Edition

In the 10 years since the publication of the first edition, the opening question 'Why write a book on women and social work?' requires a new answer. Social work and social care have given explicit recognition of the two genders, women and men, in practice and provision. Some progress in raising awareness of the gendered world we all inhabit has been made. Why then does it remain necessary to focus on women as service users and as workers, and what, given all the changes in the circumstances of women's lives, has stayed the same?

Two reasons identified in the first edition explain why a focus on women as workers and as service users should continue to be prioritised. Women have a higher risk than men of becoming service users of social services and a lower risk of becoming service users of probation, but in both situations women are vulnerable to less than adequate practice. These risks, and the contradictions and paradoxes that govern women's lives, continue to be inadequately understood.

It remains important to restate fundamentals. Gender is a total experience for women. Women do not experience life as ungendered, and nor do men. This is reflected in practice that continues to define women as wives, mothers, carers and adolescent girls, that is, in relation to their sexual behaviour and to heterosexuality as a system of social relations. Workers do not respond to women as ungendered people, but, paradoxically, gender is also invisible. When confronted, for example, with a disabled or older woman, women linguistically disappear into the categories 'disabled person', 'the elderly', 'family' or 'informal carers'. When work centres on children, 'mothers' disappear into 'parents'. These are euphemisms defining major forms of practice with women, yet debates on the role of fathers have had very little impact on the day-to-day expectations of women as mothers.

These continuities operate within a changed context. Welfare reform and economic restructuring have continued unabated throughout the decade, altering provision and practice. This has major implications for women. It is unusual for a book in this field to emphasise the relevance of macro-economic policies on practice. We have done so because the economic restructuring is determining both the shape of, and the resources for, health and social well-being. Women are being required to undertake services previously provided by the welfare state – a change of sufficient magnitude to justify a revised edition. A consequence is that the behaviour of women is being publicly presented as the cause of major social problems besetting society today. It is even more necessary today to develop women-centred practice in order to respond appropriately to women.

In this edition, we again argue for the importance of looking at women both as workers and as service users. The first edition was practice based and used the experience of women in social work and social care. We approached the writing task not through macro theory, with its orderly paradigms, but through the messiness and contradictory nature of practice with women and their/our life experience. This defines the nature of practice itself. The second edition, like the first, will be criticised for not discussing macro theories. This is deliberate. We have continued to try to do two things. The first is to translate key themes in debates – for example, the increase in uncertainty about the future, and different perspectives on the same events – into knowledge that is usable in day-to-day practice. The second is to present this in a form that enables workers to share the knowledge on which decisions are based, and which often profoundly affect women's lives and their self-image, with the women themselves. Open and accountable practice in both the care and the control aspects of our work is possible only if we avoid jargon and language that excludes all but the 'in crowd'.

Some progress has been made. A number of themes from the first edition are now seen as the components of good practice and the basis for implementing policy objectives. While they have the potential to promote women-centred practice, it is always important to be aware of how they can also be used to undermine women. We highlight four of them:

- *Responsiveness to the people who use services:* an emphasis on what works, what makes a difference, adds to the principles that we and other feminists have set out for women-centred practice. Although this is far from being achieved in general, working through how practice and provision can be more tailored to women's lives can fit within this policy initiative. The negative can be that where an individual's well-being is seen as being achieved through subordinating women's needs, responsiveness will be measured in terms of how far she can respond to the needs of others while continuing to provide the support.

- *Using the experience and expertise of the service user in reaching and resolving problems:* women-centred work has always given status to women's own experience and expertise. Practice knowledge draws on a number of sources of information or evidence – research, the experience of service users and practitioners themselves, and an understanding of the context in which we are living and working. Like life itself, practice requires judgements and compromises, often on incomplete, but the best available, information. Involving women in assessing the strengths and risks and in making these judgements is now described as user-centred practice. An emerging issue for all practitioners is the changing value placed on sources of information other than evidence from randomly controlled trials. Evidence-based practice is often, although not always, used to describe objective, scientifically based findings. Although an important source of information, in areas like social work where there are so many different factors involved in determining outcomes, other sources of information are essential resources for workers and service users when thinking how to tackle problems.

- *Open and accountable practice:* a skill now routinely required by all workers is the capacity to communicate effectively what we are doing and why. Women-centred practice has always emphasised the importance of sharing information between workers and the women using the services and involving them in judgements about risks and options. In the past 10 years, this has become a marker of good practice with all groups of service users.

- *Keeping up to date with changes in practice:* the knowledge that underpins practice and public expectation, is now a requirement of all practitioners and not an imperative only for those promoting new perspectives, as in the 1980s edition.

Macro social processes: women as problem and solution

Social work and social care address the day-to-day concerns and intimate aspects of people's lives. It is easy to forget that these are intricately woven into the wider scene of the global economy and the relationship the state creates with its citizens. There are three types of policy: social, public and economic. Social policy is about welfare and community; public policy is about how local and central government should operate, including the criminal justice system. Economic policy is about monetary issues, the labour market, growth and competitiveness within a global situation. Economic policy determines the extent and type of social and public policies within which social services agencies operate. This dimension is rarely offered on social work and social care programmes, although they are crucial to understanding social policy changes.

Women carry out their lives against a broad canvas consisting of the local and national state, the European Union and beyond. They occupy a central position in the resolution of issues identified as problematic by government and economic strategists. Major demographic, economic and political changes impacting on the lives of service users and carers today are:

- Changes in the balance of the working population, with a higher proportion of people in retirement who are living longer. A substantial proportion of older people are women; this is particularly pronounced in the 80+ group.
- Levels of unemployment, in particular among young men and women without skills or qualifications, and older men. There continues to be a disproportionate number of people from black and minority ethnic groups, and of disabled people, who are unemployed.
- Employment is an expectation for both women and men, women predominating in part-time, casual and temporary contract work.
- A policy objective for an educated and skilled workforce to maintain the UK's economic position within the rest of Europe and, along with the European Union, a determination to maintain competitiveness with other major world economies in North America, Japan and developing countries.
- Attempts by governments in Europe to reduce the proportion of public spending on welfare through the reallocation of responsibilities to provide social care between the state, individuals and their families.
- Concerns with social control and personal security because of perceived increases in violence, particularly by young men, in specific geographical areas where there are high unemployment and people living on benefits or low wages; there is also growing anxiety about violence among young women.

- Continuing political and economic negotiations between member states on European Union integration with new geographical boundaries and citizenship entitlements.

This context raises three fundamental issues for policies and practices in working with women using social service agencies:

- Women's relationships with men – and men's family rights to women and children.
- The rights of people, largely women, who become dependent on state benefits to obtain care for children or support for adults.
- The redrawing of national boundaries, restricting who may and who may not enter and reside in the UK, their entitlement to welfare and care, and their differential treatment in relation to family life. In particular this affects:

  – Women who are lone parents, particularly if they live on state benefits
  – Women who live with men but do not marry, or who marry and divorce
  – Older people/women, and disabled women
  – Immigrants and asylum-seekers.

These groups are central to the content of this book and to both care and social control functions. How the social processes stigmatising these groups will be played out in the future is difficult to predict, but by focusing on the wider context of demographic, economic and political trends, a clearer understanding can emerge of why poverty and other forms of the social exclusion of women are increasing. Understanding the impact on women of economic and political changes assists us in creating ways of responding that support and do not undermine women who use social service agencies.

Social work structures, procedures and management

Social work and care remain women's work, the majority of them having no formal qualifications. Practice continues to be undervalued while structures, procedures and management are overemphasised. However, the context in which practice and provision occur has changed dramatically. The agencies through which social work and social care operate, and those with which they collaborate, have undergone radical restructuring. In this edition, we identify how these processes of change affect what workers are expected to do. Social and care work remain women's professions, and service users and carers also remain largely women. The nature of the task in the field, group care and management, and the problems facing women, are both changing and intensifying. This revised book addresses these issues.

Qualifying education and training for the Diploma in Social Work and Vocational Qualifications (CCETSW, 1995; S/NVQs, 1996) raise issues of difference and gender. Recognition has been given to the view that research on women and practice with women needs to be included as a perspective in social work, social care, multidisciplinary and interagency work and social work education. Women are included in a number of disadvantaged social groups, and evidence from research on differences gives substance to pressures to institute practice that counters discrimination in all its forms. Even with new policies and good intentions, however, there remains a lack of ability to translate these into practice and services that positively impact on black and minority ethnic women, disabled women, older women, women with children, abused women and so on. These are themes in this second edition.

Commonalities and diversities revisited

While the issues around commonalities and diversities identified in the first edition are ongoing, these are not necessarily perceived or proceed in the same ways.

Family, employment and welfare

Over the past decade, equal opportunities in national and European governmental systems have begun to identify women in all areas of work, family life and welfare. However, the issue remains whether this identification and the policies that arise from it are leading to equality or the further oppression of women in work, family life and welfare.

In the first edition, we highlighted women and employment as an area that was difficult to include in a book on social work and social care. We saw this as part of the way in which women's role and position are constructed in our society. A decade later, rather than being an obstacle to successful womanhood and motherhood, employment is integral to it. Welfare to work and day care for children is the means of reducing dependency on benefits. In the 1980s, we wrote of 'real' work being defined as full-time and men's work. In the 1990s, the employment of women has become a central theme of public policy, and the demands for a flexible labour force have meant that the number of full-time jobs is declining, these being replaced by part-time, time-limited contracts in service industries. These traditional patterns and areas of work for women are now being extended into those of men. The attempt is to make men see these as 'real work'.

Diversities between age groups

In the first edition, differences in age groups were recognised in traditional client groups and life histories. In the economic restructuring of the past two decades, the generations of youth, adult economically active years, retirement and old age increasingly occupy differently constructed social worlds. Implications for practice are seen in the organisation of social services departments and services into children and families, and adults, the elderly being a major component of the latter group. Work with young people is increasingly focused on them as a social problem. For young women, the focus is on their sexuality and single motherhood, on an increase in female violence and on their adoption of more 'masculine' attitudes to achievement.

Disability and social exclusion

Disability leads to social exclusion. Structural arguments, such as the social model of disability, are being made by disabled people much more strongly than at the time of the first edition. These views are being translated into action using the strategies of collective action and civil disobedience. Feminist analysis and research has been found wanting, and disabled women are active in remedying this deficiency by bringing together the debate within the disabled people's movement with feminist practice and ideals. In the second edition, disabilities are being restructured as commonalities between different previously separated groups.

Polarisation around black and minority ethnic groups

Polarisation around minority groupings is another expression of social exclusion. This occurs in several ways, both in relation to the dominant group and between generations within specific communities. The different forms taken by polarisation have implications for practice and provision. Legislative changes on immigration and asylum-seekers continue to increase the vulnerability of black and minority ethnic families. The condemnation of 'political correctness' in relation to same-race placements, particularly for mixed-race children, together with economic recession, means many of the gains made in the 1960s and 70s have been reversed. Black and minority ethnic communities continue to experience higher unemployment and a disproportionately high level of physical and mental ill-health and imprisonment, and to be at greater risk of poverty than the white population. Equal opportunities in times of recession become redefined and limited in their meaning.

Structural diversity

In the first edition, we presented diversity solely as positive, as does much social care literature today. However, economic restructuring is currently separating women in ways that are difficult to bridge. Diversity remains a rich resource, but some structural changes are creating separations that are inherently divisive. For example, during slavery, white women saw black women as a sexual threat, as less than human and not women. Negative diversity was inherent in slavery as a structural form separating women from each other. Sojourner Truth's speech at the Seneca Falls Women's Suffrage meeting 'Ain't I a Woman' challenged this structure and remains a key statement on women of those times. Today, negative structural diversities in the UK and the European Union are the growing gap between rich and poor, in access to employment that is well paid and secure as against poorly paid and insecure, in adequate as against inadequate pensions, in concepts of citizenship that exclude migrants from full citizenship entitlements, in access to adequate housing, education and training, in transport and in safe and healthy living environments. This works particularly negatively against women from poorer countries and women who are black or refugees. Impairment often brings unemployment and lower earnings to disabled women, and, as community care resources become more constrained, poverty undermines independent living.

Who depends on whom?

'Who depends on whom?' is a question of fundamental relevance to understanding the paradoxes and contradictions in the lives of women. Are women dependent on men, psychologically and socially, or are men dependent on women? Or is the question of dependence much more subtle and complicated? For example, women look to men for protection from violence, yet it is men who are the most probable source of violence to women, and the closer the relationship between men and women, the more likely women are to be abused. It is illogical for women to look to the men with whom they live for protection, but this too is hidden.

Women have been portrayed in the past as economically dependent on men. This relationship is changing now that the majority of women are in employment and the number of men in full-time employment is reducing. In the 1990s, the majority of new jobs in Britain are being filled by women. These changes in the work patterns of men and women are to the disadvantage of both young men and women without qualifications or who are unskilled. Men have to respond to these changes as well. The impact of male unemployment on relationships with women and children, its link with ill-health, depression and suicide, and the use of violence and abuse against women and children all have an impact on the relationships that women have with men both within and outside the family. Holding the focus on women and their needs remains difficult. The charge that women's gains inevitably undermine men continues to be made. For example, men are portrayed as the 'new victims', discriminated against by a legislative framework of equal opportunities, a climate of political correctness that skews power too much in the direction of women and an economic climate that needs their skills.

Caring for others is equally problematic. Whether looking after husbands, children, older relatives or someone else, caring makes women financially and socially dependent on individual men or the state. Yet, at the same time, it is children, men and other dependent adults who are psychologically, and often socially and financially, dependent on women. The state is similarly dependent on women carrying out their reproductive (within due limits) and caring functions. However, this reverse dependency is invisible, hidden within an ideology that defines women as dependents of men. To reframe the dependency of women as founded on the dependence of others upon them is to reveal a more complex and valid truth. This understanding of dependency is the result of the work and analysis of women over the past two decades.

There are other well-thought-out and considered positions on the role of women and femininity that differ radically from those advanced in this text. The aim may be to counter the views of that broad grouping called 'The Women's Movement' of which we have been part, by representing women as being truly fulfilled only through marriage and motherhood. Political efforts to re-establish the traditional family of bread-earning husband and home-bound woman with children continue to surface, along with attacks on single mothers and particularly young single mothers. The past decade has seen a resurgence of a view of woman as wife and mother dependent on man as husband and father as the only socially desirable way forward. Any alternative is seen as dangerous to children and to the social status and self-respect of men, as husbands and, particularly significantly, as fathers in the family.

This dispute between women and men over their mutual relationship continues unabated, new players having entered the foray over the past decade. The Labour Party victory in 1997 heralded a new determination to reduce welfare payments, beginning with lone mothers. A reduction in welfare was presented as a 'right to work' issue even though there were more women than men in the labour market at the time of this decision (11,248 million women and 11,236 men in December 1997) and only 1 in 5 lone mothers is dependent on state benefits. This policy, based on the assumption that lone mothers are not working, makes the dependency of others on women invisible in new ways. The double and triple burden of women through informal care in the family is ignored again in 'off welfare, into work' policies. Developing good practice with women who use services, and improving the position of women workers, is adversely affected by the inability to resolve the tensions created by social changes that enable women to move forward economically, politically, socially and in the management of their personal lives. Tensions within society are experienced as conflicts within the lives of individual women, whether workers, services users or carers.

The disability movement has made a major contribution to restructuring the concept of dependence in social care through promoting a social model of disability. Nevertheless, the concept of dependence has particular meanings for disabled women and men, who are stereotyped as dependents cared for by their partners, relatives and friends. This construction has dangerous consequences where children are involved. Fear of their removal by social workers can stop disabled parents, in particular single mothers, seeking the personal assistance they require to function independently (Keith and Morris, 1996).

Visible women

Making women visible as service users, carers and workers involves a restructuring of thought and values: women must become valued in and for themselves. Making women visible also involves a greater understanding of the conflicts experienced by women and the demands made upon them, both as service users and as workers. It involves challenging current thinking about the way in which problems faced by women who use services are grouped together and about what is given priority.

The primary intention of this edition is the same as before: to make women visible as service users and as workers. The ultimate aim is to facilitate assessment and planning so that non-sexist, women-centred practice can emerge and be supported where it already exists. This involves taking into account both individual and institutional sexism. Sexism can be expressed consciously or unconsciously through individual relationships, in groups and through organisational practice and politics. Institutional sexism is the structuring of power and privilege within organisations so that one sex, by virtue of its sex, occupies a superior position. It may seem as if individuals have nothing to do with 'the way things are'. The system may appear to operate without reference to the individuals or groups that make it up. Both those who benefit and those who do not may feel powerless to intervene in the processes that maintain a system of inequality and even oppression.

We see the presentation of an alternative view on women and their problems as the first crucial step in the emergence of women-centred good practice. The second issue is to address how this can be achieved given the changing organisation of social care and the task of practitioners. In the following chapters, we weave together a woman-centred perspective on women, both as clients and as workers, with suggestions on how to begin to realise women-centred good practice and provision. The major objective is to show how a gendered approach to practice will more effectively serve the needs and wishes of both women who use services and women workers charged with the responsibility of delivering effective assistance. Achieving a gendered approach to practice also serves the organisations in which women work and people generally.

Chapter 2: Commonalities and diversities between women clients and women social workers: explores how commonalities and diversities are being restructured in provision and practice.

Chapter 3: Women, dependency and poverty: looks at women's life patterns and the awareness that is needed in order to make women-centred assessments.

Chapter 4: Women and care for children and adults: examines the impact on individuals of restructured provision and the increased transfer of responsibilities to women within the family.

Chapter 5: Living with men: tackles the sensitive issue of women's relationships with men, exploring the changing face of families, the demands on women and the implications for social work.

Chapter 6: Women, personal identity and self-esteem: returns to the centrality of personal identity and self-esteem in work with women clients and for women workers.

Chapter 7: Understanding the workplace: men, women and management: explores the implications for women workers providing direct care or services, and for women workers in management, purchasing and inspecting.

Chapter 8: Developing women-centred practice: women working with women: presents and discusses the principles and issues involved in woman-centred practice.

2

Commonalities and Diversities Between Women Clients and Women Social Workers

Racism, the belief in the inherent superiority of one race over all others and thereby the right to dominance. Sexism, the belief in the inherent superiority of one sex over another and thereby the right of dominance. Ageism, Heterosexism, Elitism, Disablism, Classism. (Lorde, 1984, p. 115)

We agree with Audre Lorde when she said:

> It is a lifetime pursuit for each one of us to extract these distortions from our living at the same time as we recognise, reclaim, and define those differences upon which they are imposed. For we have all been raised in a society where those distortions were endemic within our living. (1984, p. 116)

Chapter 2 develops the themes of commonalities and diversities between women. It begins by exploring generic issues, with the aim of relating these themes to practice and the organisation of services. This is followed by commonalities between women workers and service users, and their implications for practice. Diversities between women workers and service users are explored next, in particular employment and unemployment, black and minority ethnic women, disabled women and age. Feeling powerful and powerless and the social and personal conditions associated with these responses are presented as part of recognising and acknowledging commonalities and differences between women workers and service users. The centrality of recognising diversity through commonality for women-centred practice is then introduced.

Stability and change since the 1980s

The 1980s saw an increase in the social work and social care literature on commonalities and diversities between the lives of women. Published work on racism and how it and sexism can be tackled is considerable (for example Dominelli and McLeod, 1989; Ahmad, 1990; Phillipson, 1992). Demonstrating an understanding of sources of discrimination and the capacity to challenge them through practice and service delivery has become a requirement for qualification. Considerable steps forward have been made, but the context in which our understanding of how common-alities and diversities affect our lives and work has changed and is still changing rapidly. Disabled women or women with learning difficulties have rightly criticised us for ignoring these perspectives (Williams, 1992; Morris, 1996; Power House, 1996; Hemmings and Morris, 1997).

Yet other patterns persist. While women workers are aware of gender perspectives, there remains a reluctance to think about commonalities and diversities between ourselves and the people who use services. An emphasis on citizenship and consumerism has not shifted the deeply ingrained separation between those who use and those who provide services. Targeting scarce resources through assessment and care management, financial controls and organisational procedures has meant that, in the statutory sector, opportunities for working alongside people who use services may have declined in spite of the rhetoric of empower-ment and user-centred services. Ironically, targeting greatest need has meant an even greater pathologising of people in order to qualify for state funded provision.

Open, non-stigmatising services are declining at the same time as there is a growing emphasis on the need for supportive and preventative services. Some open provision still exists in the voluntary sector, but the reliance on contract rather than core funding as the primary means of ensuring quality means that this is often vulnerable to financial cuts. Opportunities to work alongside people are available in parts of the private and voluntary sectors and in organisations that are led by users or carers. Wherever these exist, women can use them to develop practice that is sensitive to issues of gender, race, disability and sexuality. In response to changes in the personal social services and in the wider social context, practice has to re-recognise and re-conceptualise commonalities and diversities between women, as women remain the majority of both workers and the people who use services.

Generic issues

Changes in the provision of community and child care have reinforced the divisions between people who need access to provision. Most local authority social services have reorganised into separate sections for children and families, and for adults. Although a few are providing community-based, open access provision, the trend towards specialism by user group is reinforced in the organisation of the private and voluntary sectors, where services tend to focus on particular groups of users or carers. The main groupings are:

- Children, young people and families
- Older people
- Disabled people
- People with learning difficulties
- People with mental distress
- Juvenile and other offenders.

People are put in particular categories that do not address how one aspect of their lives interacts with other dimensions, their gender, race or sexuality. For black and minority ethnic women who are disabled, ungendered categorisation ignores the complex interactions that determine their experience: 'it's the totality that counts at the end of the day' (Vernon, 1996).

There are two issues: contracting for services and the fragmentation of service delivery. Contracting for services here, as in the USA, is pushing service delivery into specifically categorised provision based on identifying which particular groups of service users under which conditions should be the beneficiaries of state resources, irrespective of the sector through which provision is to be made (Smale, 1996). While contracting for services has its advantages through setting out what is required, the fears of smaller local groups that they will lose out to larger well-resourced organisations has proved well founded. Black, minority ethnic and women's groups still find that they are at a disadvantage in the tendering and contracting process (Butt and Box, 1997). The level of administrative demands inherent in contracting, and the emphasis on traditional accountability systems, provides a strong push for purchasers of care to go for block contracts with the larger traditional organisations. A second disadvantage for smaller, local organisations is that the mechanisms and experience to undertake the consultations required for both community care and children's plans may be lacking. This can mean that the perspectives and interests of key stakeholders in community and child care can be overlooked or poorly represented (Statham, 1996).

The fragmentation of service delivery has been created by the policy of expanding the number of providers in the private and voluntary sectors. Financial incentives put in place during the 1980s succeeded to the extent that the majority of residential care is now provided in the private sector. Local authorities continue to divest themselves of residential provision, and there is a growing, although much slower, development of home care services in the private and voluntary sectors. This mixed economy of care has two key implications. First, there are a multiplicity of providers instead of the majority of services being provided through the local authority. The social market, as this is called, also carries within it the creation of divisions between groups of people that often make more sense in organisational and budgetary terms than in recognising the commonalities emerging through the shared experience of gender. Second, providers tend to specialise, and contracts for one person with high levels of need can involve several providers and include inputs from all sectors as well as from relatives and neighbours.

There is an issue here about coherence and how the whole context of the person's life is kept in focus. Attention is on certain aspects of problems while ignoring other areas of commonalities between individuals contained within these classifications. For example, most people who use social services are working class, poor and often live within particular geographical areas that lack resources and where other people on low wages or benefits also live (Hills, 1995). Women's lives are constrained by violence, racial abuse and a lack of access to facilities, transport and social support for their caring responsibilities. All easily fall out of focus because of the fragmented way in which need is categorised and prioritised. The care manager's responsibility is very often on the coordination of the total package that has been devised to deal with those problems within statutory responsibilities and that meet eligibility criteria.

There is a logic in excluding from social care classifications the categories of women, men, the poor and the unemployed. The definition of service user groups rests on categories of people or problems for which central and local government overtly accepts some responsibility for their protection or control. These responsibilities are formalised through social policy, legislation and statutory requirements relating to social work, social care and probation. These can be a source of difficulty for many people who need personal assistance or care; for example, where a family has to cope with the ill-health of the mother, her needs and those of the children can be seen as separate rather than as interlocking. The same dangers exist if an elderly person with dementia is looked after in a family where there are young people. These separations are structured into the current system of provision, although everyone in the network of the service user is affected by his or her behaviour and needs (Smale *et al.*, 1994). Work on gender requires attention to these 'interfaces' if it is to be relevant to the totality of women's lives.

State-defined divisions do not necessarily make sense as a way of categorising people. For example, disability is a meaningless grouping to an anthropologist (Oliver, 1983), and its use as a category has individualised impairments and led to the medicalisation of disabled people's lives (Begum, 1996). The disability movement seeks inclusion in the public world and relationships, not exclusion by category (Morris, 1993a, 1993b, 1996). A further source of difficulty is that the vast majority of social care for young people and adults is provided through family, relatives and friends, with social services provision and resources marginal to the enterprise. All too often, categories can become rigid and place statutory resourced provision in the centre of the analysis rather than as a significant, but very limited, contribution to the mass of social care that is provided by families and in communities. Most of this care is provided by women, who often assume a double or triple burden by taking on this work.

Community groups are more likely to find common ground around such issues as poverty, racism, women, unemployment or making estates a safer and better resourced place for people to live. Access to participation in, and contributing to, the community comes through housing, transport, employment, income and having supportive networks and access to personal assistance. Becoming labelled as a service user is often a direct result of not having access to resources or dependable support at times of crisis or difficulty (Smale *et al.*, 1999). The vast majority of service users and carers want to avoid becoming a social service category, in order to live as independent a life as possible (Harding and Beresford, 1996; Beresford and Turner, 1997).

A growing number of people are buying their own social care and personal assistance, at least for some period of time. This will increase with the ability to provide state finances directly to service users who meet eligibility criteria, to select and employ their own personal assistants (Community Care (Direct Payments) Bill, 1996). People with access to private income or state funds can use or set up alternative forms of provision. These trends may begin to alter the balance of power, including the definition of what outcomes are desirable, towards service users and carers. In parallel with these developments is the access that some women have acquired through well-paid employment: they can then purchase social care for the children and adults for whom they are responsible. The relationships that workers have with service users are often very complicated.

Commonalities

Within the complex and changing form of service delivery, women workers and service users continue to share commonalities. They group around being female, their relationships with men, children, living within the family, employment and working conditions, and more general cultural expectations and pressures on women. These commonalities offer both a resource and a strength for practice. We suggest that it is only through a recognition of commonalities that a true assessment of the situation facing women clients and user-centred practice can emerge.

In social work and social care, there is no stress on commonality between service users and workers. The emphasis on citizenship and consumer rights to information and to make complaints does little to alter a basis distinction between those who purchase or provide and those who use services that are resourced from central or local government funding. As an increasing number of workers becomes responsible for older relatives as well as children (Balloch *et al.*, 1995, 1998), the failure to recognise these commonalities becomes more problematic for practice. In spite of inside knowledge of the system, it is often difficult to transfer their expertise as worker into that required by themselves as service user. Becoming a service user is to learn through experience of the fragmentation, inflexibility and partiality of available service and the conflicting social expectations and emotional pull.

We continue to come across commonalities between workers and service users more by accident than as part of our formal training and education. When this occurs, we can feel surprise, shock, shame and denial. To recognise commonalties is to raise fears of overidentification, of overinvolvement, thereby producing an inability accurately and 'objectively' to assess the service users' problems. These responses can negate important commonalities such as gender, class, minority ethnic group, disability, sexuality, culture, being a carer and other differentiating characteristics between people. As a result, there can be a failure to work collaboratively with service users or carers and to develop shared understandings. Insights gained from the context and day-to-day experiences of women can be underused when workers and service users or carers meet. When intervention is aimed at change, a focus on commonalties can assist in identifying areas of conflict within women's social networks that must be negotiated. Maintaining a distance between workers and users contrasts with organisations led by service users and carers in which commonality of experience is the base from which services are built and their outcomes evaluated.

Identifying common experience as a powerful force for change and growth is a key feature of the women's, the black liberation and the disability movements and remains a vital means of structuring and analysing the experience of disadvantaged groups. It is sometimes assumed that accepting the people's definitions of their needs for care or personal assistance will lead to an escalation of demand, even though evidence is to the contrary (Levin and Moriarty, 1994; Pitkeathley, 1995). Collective support groups make decisions and manage conflicts that are no less difficult than those of social service agencies. A framework of valuing experience and respect for civil rights does not rely on distance and difference, which is often structured into the relationships between those who use and those who provide services.

Workers intervene in the personal and often intimate area of people's lives irrespective of the structural category in which they are based. It is for this reason that the capacity to become self-aware is valued in social work and social care. Understanding ourselves, our values and attitudes, and the impact that our style of work has on others is regarded as an important part of training and professional development. Recognising and understanding gendered experience is an essential part of becoming sufficiently self-aware to provide user-centred services. The impact of the ways in which workers behave, and the attitudes they convey, on the lives of the people who use services cannot be underestimated.

Users and carers consistently identify the worker's style and relationship with them as crucial factors in determining the quality of service received. They assume that they have a right to expect competence and for the worker to do the job in ways that promote the confidence and self-esteem of the people who use services (Harding and Beresford, 1996). The merits and demerits of self-disclosure are rarely discussed in the literature on counselling and interviewing, but gender, like age or being black or having an obvious impairment, is not a characteristic that we can choose when or where to disclose. These characteristics are not disclosed by working at the service user's or carer's pace: they are visible from the first contact. A women-centred approach to practice recognises that what we share with other women is part of the assumptions built into relationships with users and carers. The same applies to the differences or diversities between us (Robinson, 1995).

In many interactions with women using services, what we share and how we differ is usually complicated rather than straightforward. We may share some experiences, such as living with men or children, or caring for an older person, but not others, for example impairment. A common difference will be between the woman worker who has employment, an adequate income and access to education and training, compared with most women service users, who will be poor and have few qualifications or recognised skills. These differences between workers and users are not always as marked. Care workers are often poorly paid, have few qualifications and are subject to poorer conditions of employment than social workers. Understanding the life patterns of women and the diversities between women are essential when developing relationship-building skills, including with colleagues in our own and other organisations. The quality of interpersonal interactions is fundamental to the provision of a service. Mistaken assumptions or oversimplified approaches to gendered experience and identity can not only distort assessment and provision, but also deny the individuality, uniqueness and options available to women.

There are a number of key commonalties that arise from women's basic life experience, which we will explore in subsequent chapters. These are:

- The problematic impact on women of female life experience
- The public–private division of life through managing the double load of home and paid work
- Women's relationships with men and the impact on our private and our public worlds
- Being mothers and caring for adults
- Women's relationships with women
- The influence, more generally, of society and social changes on women, including the way in which the economic and social consequences of divorce are being handled.

While commonalities exist whether or not women are wives, mothers, carers, disabled or non-disabled, in employment or unemployed, they operate on different dimensions:

- Between the service user or carer and the worker
- Between women workers
- Between women generally, irrespective of age, stage, impairment, sexuality, class, minority ethnic group and reproductive history.

Implementing women-centred practice

The first task in women-centred practice is consciously to recognise the commonalities we share as women, and the second, rather than to ignore or marginalise these, to incorporate them as visible parts of our practice. As well as recognising the strengths our gender brings us, we also have to be sufficiently self-aware to be unafraid when service users or carers face us with the vulnerabilities we share with them as women. One way to bring commonalities into the open in our thinking and planning is to make them explicit in some way, beginning, for example, by drawing up an individual or collective list using examples from our own lives and those of the people who use our services. No list is ever complete. As our lives change and develop, we acquire new understanding that then becomes a conscious part of our practice, and our list may expand.

Although in most working groups in social care the crude stereotyping of black and white women has ceased because of the implementation of equal opportunities policies, more subtle examples still persist. Conversations about gender or race that do not 'fit' equal opportunities policies have become part of the separate communications patterns of men and women, as in the phrase 'I wouldn't say this in front of the sisters (as assertive women colleagues are sometimes called), but...'. A similar separatist culture is maintained in relation to black and disabled colleagues. Clearly, this does not apply to everyone, or every office, but these are examples of parallel cultures – the official and the informal. It is inevitable that this ambivalence is picked up by the people who use services and is one of the reasons that service users comment on the failure of workers to hear what they are saying about themselves and their experience. The attitude of workers is sometimes found to be condescending and patronising (Morris, 1996; Hemmings and Morris, 1997).

A lack of understanding, whether from a backlash or from ignorance of the effects of discrimination, results in additional stress for black and white women. Racist behaviour and a lack of support from white colleagues is still an all too frequent experience of black workers. In a survey by Balloch *et al.,* three-quarters of the sample of black workers had experienced racism from service users or their relatives, and almost one-half from their colleagues (1995, 1998). The failure of colleagues to treat these incidents seriously was experienced as a significant source of stress for black workers.

For men, the task is different. In the statutory sector, provision for children, families and people with mental distress and severe learning difficulties is more likely to be managed by men than women. The men in residential care are more likely to work with children and very few work in domiciliary care in the statutory sector. The importance of men having a gender perspective is crucial to the provision of user-centred provision. Men need to learn to become more comfortable with gender deviance and diversity among themselves before they can make the leap towards understanding women. Experiential resources are available within their personal and work experiences to achieve this in their practice.

We suggest four useful exercises for men:

1. *To get information about men who take primary care responsibilities for children and adults and what their experience is.*
2. *To identify their attitudes and behaviours to male service users, carers and their own colleagues who are involved in tasks usually undertaken by women.* For example, where an older person needs care, this is usually provided by the spouse or a partner of either gender (Sinclair *et al.,* 1990). In addition, 7.4 per cent of one-parent families are headed up by men (Haskey, 1991). Some of these men are colleagues. Providing intimate and personal care is a regular feature of residential, day and domiciliary care, provision in which men are working. We know that women in home care can be very satisfied with the work they do and its value, but men are much less likely to express this view (Balloch *et al.,* 1995).
3. *How they view themselves and the tasks they carry out in the home that are usually performed by women.* In spite of substantial changes in the lives of a minority of men, like the well-publicised house fathers, the majority of household and child care tasks are still carried out by women irrespective of whether or not they are in dual earner households (ONS, 1992).
4. *To identify the patterning of masculinity among young men.* While some take the macho-male path, Wilkinson and Mulgan (1995) argue

that others are adopting softer and more caring values. They contrast this with the 'masculinatisation' of some young women who seek success, their own enjoyment and risk-taking.

In recent years there has been a growing number of groups for male workers, aiming to create greater gender awareness. Groups for male workers can improve practice through extending self-awareness and understanding in their work with women, and by providing support to men who are trying to develop more women-centred practice either as practitioners or managers. There is a sense among some men that women are gaining too much power as a growing number move into management positions. In an effort to move towards a more sophisticated understanding of gender, men need to find ways of drawing into their conscious practice what they see as commonalities between women.

Diversities

Diversity exists between women in the same categories in which commonalities are found, that is:

- Service users and carers
- Women workers
- Women generally.

Diversities, however, are frequently not readily apparent except in stereotypical ways. The task of identification cannot be undertaken without first asking a number of questions, such as:

- Is an understanding of power relations basic to working with diversity?
- What is the significance of diversity in the way in which race, gender, class, disability, age and the expression of sexuality interact with each other?
- Are these diversities natural qualities or socially determined attributes?

All these are important questions to which there are no easy or simple answers. They need debate and discussion; there will be disagreements and conflicts. Over time, we may change our minds because of new experience or knowledge. It is important to make these opinions a conscious part of our assessment and interventions because they form part of the theories we use to make sense and order out of what we see and hear. There is no neutrality or objective fact in this complex arena of our work, but there are different and conflicting perceptions of social problems and how they might be resolved. Where practice is not woman centred, there is a serious danger that the perspective that dominates will be that of the white, non-disabled man, because of the power imbalance that operates both within and outside the family and workplace.

Employment and unemployment

Whether a woman is in employment or not is a major diversity and may make the difference between living in or out of poverty. The contribution that husbands made to the overall household income fell in the 1980s, and if more women had not taken up employment, the gap between rich and poor families would be greater than it already is. In the 1990s, 1 in 3 children live in poverty. Lone motherhood is still a major source of exclusion from employment. In 1992, 42 per cent of lone parents were in employment, and this figure has not changed much since the early 1980s. One-third of all lone parents are just managing, but with escalating debts. While one-third of these are living in severe hardship, not every lone mother or father is able to work because of the young age of their children or the need to provide stability for the children after separation or divorce. The proportion of single mothers in employment is considerably lower than that of married or cohabiting women (Utting, 1995). Social policies such as reducing welfare entitlements, day care and welfare to work programmes to encourage single mothers to return to work are intended to alter this balance. There are also a number of families where no family members are in employment. The idea of 'work rich and work poor' is used to describe these differences. Overcoming exclusion from unemployment is least problematic when some family members are already in work.

Women's increasing participation in the labour market and the reduction in the number of full-time 'male' jobs is changing the economic basis of the relationship between men and women. Whereas in the past young men had greater access to full-time work and a higher income, they are now more likely to be unemployed or to be in poorly paid, insecure work. Although unemployment among 16–25-year-olds is higher than that among other age groups, young men are 6 per cent more likely than young women to be unemployed. Access to employment now influences the age at which young women have their first child. A significant number of young women from less-privileged backgrounds and without work qualifications are having children independently at an earlier age than their counterparts in better paid work, who are concentrating on developing their careers (Rogers and Rogers, 1996). However, the average age of the never-married mother is now 25 years, and only 1 in 10 single mothers is under 20 (Burghes and Brown, 1995).

The majority of women who use social services provision are unemployed, and those in paid work are likely to be in low-paid, insecure jobs and to have poor conditions of employment irrespective of the hours they work. Training and professional status, which the vast majority of the workforce do not enjoy, bring social workers a higher earning capacity, equal pay, greater access to education and training, better conditions of work and a job that allows greater flexibility in planning and organising work (Ford *et al.*, 1998). However, a sense of well-being in employment may not be how workers experience their employment, but when compared with the employment options open to many service users, the job remains in many senses privileged, if pressed. Adequate pay and qualifications give social workers access to decent housing and transport, and opens up new options for them.

Persistent reorganisations of departments and local government have made employment in social service agencies less secure. Rather than people leaving, their jobs are changing around them. If movement is taking place, it is likely to be because of redundancy or between qualifying and finding employment. The forces for restructuring the social services will continue for the foreseeable future. Some women will have difficulties returning to work after a period away, for example after the birth of a child, when caring for a relative, as a result of illness or because they are tied to a particular geographical area by a partner's work or family responsibilities. There are geographical variations in the availability of employment and the level of remuneration, but the problems faced are unlikely to be as great as those of many people who use services. Although still small by comparison with other areas of industry and commerce, unemployment is growing in social work and social care, as is the casualisation of employment through time-limited contracts. Men are more likely than women to work full time and, when they do, to be better paid than women, who are less likely to occupy senior positions (Balloch *et al.*, 1995).

The restructuring of industry through the 1980s has produced more opportunities for women, but it has not dismantled occupational segregation. In the statutory social services, women predominate in the total workforce. Apart from social workers, women are concentrated in residential and home care, and share with other women employment in largely segregated occupations.

Black and minority ethnic women

The different experiences of black and white women are another source of diversity. The degree of diversity is particularly acute when black workers meet white service users and carers. Combining gender differences with race, for example white women clients with black men workers, or black women service users or carers with white men social or care workers, intensifies diversity. A multiplicity of barriers exist for disabled black and minority ethnic women. These result from the combination of disablism, racism and sexism. Black workers also experience a status contradiction from being black and holding power as a worker. There can be a conflict between their loyalties to their community and to the organisation, whose services may not be as ethnically appropriate or sensitive as stated policies have indicated (Butt, 1994). The number of men or women from black and minority ethnic groups in senior management positions in social services still remains very low. Evidence from research into black and minority ethnic groups in the local authority social service workforce indicates that a significant number feel unsupported by their colleagues and managers when they experience racism (Balloch, 1995).

While the day-to-day lives of poor black and poor white women within the family, combining paid work with domestic labour and caring for children and adults, are commonalities, racism creates a diversity. Black women have to live with a sharper sense of the contradiction that the family is both oppressive to them and at the same time a refuge from racism. For a number of black people, immigration controls mean separation from their children and husbands, wives and fiancées. The aim is to unite the family (European Women's Lobby, 1993). Black and minority ethnic women also have to cope with greater levels of unemployment, particularly of young people and men, the criminalisation of young black males, poorer housing and lower income.

The recognition of commonalities and the easy development of companionship between black and white women is restricted by the knowledge of the power that white women hold and their different histories and cultures. Black women describe the conditions they have to place on their feelings and commitment to white women as almost like having to 'hedge your bets' because racism could intervene at any time. Greater intellectual understanding of the nature of personal and institutional racism will not remove this fact at present. 'White women are born with it [power] and the greater their economic privilege the greater their power' (Moraga and Anzaldua, 1981, p. 62), or again, 'Within the community of women, racism is a reality force within my life as it is not within yours (Lorde, 1981, p. 97). The continuing struggle to identify this imbalance of power and the effect it has on the relationships between women has fallen mainly on black women. Our language also excludes: to speak of 'black people' and of 'women' makes black women invisible (Ahmad, 1990).

Recognising commonalities means understanding that there are areas in which black women's struggles and issues are different from white women's. For Afro-Caribbean women, slavery meant that white women saw black women as a sexual threat while expecting them to labour in the home and fields. Most white women, like most white men, did not oppose slavery. The triangular trade in slaves, raw materials and manufactured goods between Africa, the Americas and Britain produced great wealth for the British Isles for several centuries. While there was a social movement, including white women abolitionists, to abolish slavery, we should not ignore the major contribution made through the sacrifice and suffering of black people, or the fact that slavery remains part of their history, literature, music, poetry and memory. In Asia and the Indian subcontinent, white women were similarly a part of the imperialist power structure and took it into their relationships with Asian women. A few notable exceptions prove the rule and do not erase the general historical experience (hooks, 1981). Black and minority ethnic women today still do not, in the main, see white women as major allies in their struggles against the impact of racism on their own and their families' lives (Bernard, 1997).

Black women often decide to prioritise being black even though, in terms of experience, it is hard to separate out being a woman and being black. Black women are acutely conscious of the impact of discrimination on their children at school, on young men and adult males in the world of employment and on the construction of black men as abusers, as aggressive, as criminals (Butt and Box, 1997). This feeds the power of white people, particularly white men. The distribution between people of the care and control functions of welfare is unequal. Black people are more likely to experience social control aspects of provision than they are care. This persists in spite of improvements in implementing policies to provide more ethnically sensitive and appropriate services, and is evidenced by the disproportionately larger number of young and adult black male offenders in the criminal justice system, a similar trend being seen in sectioning for mental health admissions.

The family is an important means by which black women and men, children and young people, can gain a positive image of themselves and avoid the powerlessness that comes from the negative valuation placed on them by external sources. The dynamics of racism continue to be not well understood by white women. They often fail to recognise the need to develop the 'street sense and skills' required for black people to survive and have a positive identity. White people, including women, usually underestimate the strengths and resources of black and minority ethnic communities as a major source of support. Decisions about the priority to give to gender by black and minority ethnic women are mediated by this knowledge.

Disabled women

Disabled women feel betrayed and excluded by feminists. Jenny Morris (1995, 1996) points out how disabled women have not had their perspective properly addressed within the women's movement, in feminist literature or in research. They have been absent from work on domestic violence and abuse, including institutional abuse. This experience has only become visible through the writings and research of disabled women.

The social model of disability provides a framework that can be combined with the social construction of gender to understand how gender and disability interact to create the specific experience of disabled women. Disabled feminists have put the dimension of personal relationships into the social model of disability, arguing that the personal is political and that relationships are integral to the way in which we, as women, define ourselves and our identity (Keith, 1996). The community care debate takes on a specific significance for disabled mothers. Discussions about the needs of young carers often portray the disabled parent as a burden, the reason young people take on responsibilities for care beyond that expected at their age. This diverts attention from the needs of disabled parents for support to enable them to carry out parenting functions. Demands on young people are the result of an absence of appropriate support for disabled parents, ignoring the fact that the majority of young carers still see themselves as receiving care from their parents. The roles have not reversed in the ways often suggested (Keith and Morris, 1996).

Age groups

There are now major differences between the life patterns of younger women and the older generation. Whereas for many of us in our fifties and sixties, options may have been limited by a lack of access to education or the expectation that mothers with young children would not work, there was some clarity about different pathways and their consequences. Taking time out to look after children or dependent adults meant difficulties in returning to employment at the same level and conditions; it took longer for women than for male colleagues to reach senior positions, and women had lesser pension rights. For professional women, job security was assumed up to retirement. In the 1980s and 90s, a number of people have taken early retirement as part of 'downsizing' or as a means of escaping increases in work pressures and demands. While this is not an option for many working-class women, it has been taken by women in the professions whose pensions are sufficient to exercise this option. Although this route is closing in the 1990s, and women's retirement age will equal that of men early in the 2000s, early retirement can provide a welcome escape from increasingly heavy work demands and redefined job descriptions. An adequate pension can give the opportunity to focus on particular areas of professional activity by becoming self-employed and to alter the pace of work demands. Other women have been removed reluctantly and suffer both economic and professional isolation.

For younger women and men alike, there are fewer clear-cut career paths or life patterns. The task is coping with uncertainty and change, including the expectation of facing periodic unemployment, as industries and businesses restructure and relocate, including moving between countries. Coping with uncertainty and fluctuating income is a life skill young people are having to acquire. Women as a group are no longer the 'flexible buffer' of the labour supply. New labour reserves are appearing in the form of young people and older people through early retirement. Young women are taking risks different from those which older women faced in their youth, whose key choices were whether to pursue education and employment, whether to be sexually active outside marriage, and what degree of economic independence from family and men they desired.

There has been a shift in the age group where poverty predominates. From the 1980s, this has moved from the elderly to young people and families, to the extent that, in the mid-1990s, families with children find themselves on the wrong side of the widening gap between rich and poor. At the end of the twentieth century, the expectation is that employment will be a continuing feature in the lives of women, and employment patterns currently thought of as 'atypical' are likely to become more routine in the lives of both men and women.

Feeling powerful – feeling powerless

Women service users and carers do not meet workers as equals. In focusing on commonalities, the power differences between them must not be forgotten. However, this is not a simple dichotomy, although the powerful worker versus the powerless woman using services is a theme of many discussions. A second way in which a power–powerlessness dichotomy is organised is to experience oneself, as a woman worker, as powerless and the agency as powerful. Although we all feel like this at times, this crude division of powerful–powerless is an oversimplification. Equality of power is not how it feels to people using services, particularly when statutory control powers are used in child protection or mental health, or when the worker acts as a gatekeeper to resources. Nor is it an accurate analysis when thinking in categories of:

- Service users or carers and social work and care staff and their organisation

or when considering the relationships between:

- Specific service users or carers and an individual worker or team
- Specific workers and their line managers.

In the past, there was a focus on individual pathology, problems and failures, on the weaknesses or deficits of a person, group or community. The move towards user-centred provision and the emphasis on citizenship has given a strong philosophical push to emphasising existing strengths and supports available to individuals in social networks.

Assessment criteria can operate against this when the test is to prove that they fall into the 'worst of all' category to receive a service. Community work and community-based practice emphasise mobilising resources and strengths in collectivities, in social networks and among their individual members. Power shifts and changes hands; the need is for negotiation and the resolution of conflicts. To practise in this way means that workers have to identify their own sources of power and weakness in different situations and to share their expertise with the people who use services and make up community groups or networks.

There are disadvantages in being a professional worker that are not necessarily shared with service users or carers. These include the inability to acknowledge publicly any sexuality but heterosexuality, the difficulty in acknowledging some political opinions and activities, or lifestyles that deviate from those of the heterosexual nuclear family, and the attitudes colleagues and managers may have towards disabilities and mental distress. For black workers, being a representative of the state, particularly when there is conflict, for example between black organisations and the agency, can create conflicting demands. Workers are mostly seen as powerful, and the people who use services as powerless. In reality, many of the same disadvantages may be experienced by women workers.

A number of factors based on life experience may function to restrict the acknowledgement of the dichotomy of power and powerlessness. These are:

- Life opportunities and experiences associated with social class
- Guilt arising from the advantages brought by professional occupation, which can create social distance from those using the services and the ignoring of commonalities between women
- Relationships between women and men.

Men still hold most of the power in the family, even when they are living outside it, and in the workplace as managers. Who then is more oppressed in her personal relationship: the middle-class woman worker or the working-class woman service user or carer? Gender and class interact in complex ways, and women workers have the same problems in their relationships with men as do the women who use services. For example, some of us have been sexually abused (Commission of Inquiry into the Prevention of Child Abuse, 1996), while others have been or are in violent relationships with men, or are continually negotiating on money and children with men, including those who no longer live with us. The worker may move from being confident and powerful in their work to being less in control at home and face problems similar to those of the people she has been working with during the day.

Women and access to economic resources

Many middle-class women would be unable to maintain their economic position on their own. In the main their husbands' incomes are essential to their class position. Furthermore, even when women earn, they often earn less than men, and even when they earn the equivalent of the man or more, they may not have control over their own incomes (Homer *et al.*, 1984). Women's work patterns tend to be concentrated in the less-secure areas of part-time and time-limited work. Most workers will earn more than service users who are in employment. Carers' incomes and pensions tend to be adversely affected when they take on home-based responsibilities above a certain level. Social work and social care still provide access to a professional career for women from working-class backgrounds. Their economic independence relies on job security and reductions in the resources – including the human resources – available to meet social needs. For women workers, a loss of earning power means becoming dependent, directly on men or indirectly through the state.

Age and power

Power and powerlessness affect women of all ages, but in a society where youthfulness is valued and identified with vigour, beauty and creativity, and where downsizing in organisations includes early retirement packages, ageing brings specific difficulties. Younger women, in contrast, suffer restricted access to benefits and higher levels of unemployment even though the majority of new jobs in the UK, now and up to the beginning of the twenty-first century, are expected to be filled by women.

There is a danger that the richness of older women's lives will ignored. Women are the majority of the very elderly, and in the debates on funding long-term care, they can be seen as a burden on the young and the state (Harding *et al.*, 1996). The paradox is that while women provide the majority of care for older people, they are also the largest group of those likely to require that care. Although the vast majority of elderly people are fit and healthy, the incidence of disability and illness increases with age. Women over 75 are most likely to live alone or not in a family setting, and the majority of people over the age of 85 are women. The increasing emphasis on providing for our own care means that all of us, except women who are economically wealthy, will become vulnerable to requiring long-term care and should therefore be concerned about its availability, cost and quality.

Black and minority ethnic groups and racism

Black women experience the powerlessness associated with racism, which can be from some service users, carers or colleagues, or be the structural racism of the organisations that they work in and collaborate with. The criminalisation of black males may make black women fear contact with sources of potential support from predominantly white organisations. The particular pressures and constraints on black women, their families and communities reduces their power to call on much-needed resources.

Sexuality and homophobia

Because of homophobia, heterosexual women are seen as powerful and lesbian women as powerless. It is particular noticeable that only the women who have directly experienced racism and homophobia or discrimination based on disability are fully aware of the damage that this does to women. The shared experience of discrimination, although of different origins, contains the potential to transfer an understanding of its impact.

Disability and able-bodiedness

The dichotomy of non-disabled and disabled similarly creates a framework for constructing powerfulness and powerlessness. This is particularly profound where the analysis of the impact of impairment is based on a medical rather than a social model. Disability is then seen as inherent in the person. It becomes the person's responsibility to cope in a world constructed in ways that excludes her or him from participation. How resources are rationed between community-based and residential provision crucially affects disabled women's access to independence. A financial limit on community care packages means that disabled women and men can be forced to leave their homes and families.

Recognising differences

An awareness of differences arises out of direct experience and sharing what we learn with and from each other. It requires a consciousness that this learning is important and relevant to social work and social care tasks. Above all, it requires moving from polemic and ideological statements and positioning to the hard work of learning about and valuing the differences in the detail of our day-to-day lives. This detail is crucial whether the focus is personal relationships or civil disobedience. It ranges from understanding that the protest tactics used by disabled people, such as chaining themselves to buses and lorries, could create high risks for mental health survivors because the same behaviour could be interpreted as a sign of illness rather than as an exercise of strength (Lindow, 1994).

There is a danger that in a predominantly white, heterosexual workforce, dominated by the non-disabled and middle class, certain differences are given more attention than others. Income, relationships with men and education, rather than disability, minority ethnic membership or age, are emphasised. How this particular woman's situation and problems differ from one's own and those of other women should be part of assessment irrespective of the route that brought her into contact with the worker. Differences in status, power, role, lifestyle, impairment, race, culture, sexuality, education, employment possibilities, access to community resources, the nature of their social network, the degree of stigma and hope are elements in the differentiation of the woman worker and the woman using services. Many of these diversities cannot be accessed through a questioning and form-filling approach to assessment (Smale *et al.*, 1994) but are essential components in professional assessment and practice based on skills of collaboration. But how is the recognition of diversities aided by the recognition of similarities?

Recognising diversity through commonality

Recognising commonalities affects the approach of the worker and the style of relationship she develops with service users and carers. While it may appear paradoxical, recognising commonalities gives the worker the psychological distance necessary to see the woman in her own setting and life experience. The worker is given both the space and the theoretical perspective to enable her to recognise how the forces of society in general and of personal relationships in particular affect her responses and the practical responses of a woman using services.

Without a process of recognising first commonalities and then differences, the danger of stereotyping women as 'not coping', 'at risk' or 'incapable', and the worker as 'coping' and 'invulnerable', is far greater. The process creates and maintains psychological distance and results in objectifying the woman, seeing her in terms of her social roles rather than as a person in her own right. The recognition of the woman's own strength, powers and ability to understand the sources of her problems and how they might be resolved is inhibited by a procedural approach rather than a reflective assessment and response.

The greater insight that comes from the recognition of diversities in the context of commonality is rooted in a genuine contact with and perception of the other person. Workers who are open to this process and knowledge are less likely to impose either their own stereotypes, their own personal solutions or use service-led responses. They will have the analytical framework to make an assessment focused on the woman and her social network, and will be more likely to facilitate groups for women who have common life experiences. They will be aware of the strength that can be drawn from women sharing expertise and using this as a resource. Ensuring that there are ways in which women using services can feed into policy, planning, assessment and the evaluation of outcomes and their quality is a key task to be achieved. We must not lose sight of the fact that all of this experience is gendered and that the majority of people who use services continue to be women.

Involvement in groups and the planning and development of provision gives women, both individually and collectively, greater power over their own lives. They are less likely to despair within themselves, to see themselves silently and secretly as the only person – whether worker or service user/carer – not coping among their Amazonian colleagues and friends. The potential to recreate the definition of reality and what will 'make a difference' is possessed by women workers. Non-sexist practice becomes possible when the recognition of commonalities is its cornerstone.

People using services are consistent in emphasising the importance to them of the quality of the relationship with the worker (Harding and Beresford, 1996). This can be underestimated in a culture that stresses that which can be measured in terms of cost or time spent, or the number of people assessed or receiving a service (Kearney, 1995). Recognising commonalities encourages empathy and authenticity in relationships. Both are central to women-centred practice and to avoiding victim-blaming responses. Empathy and authenticity facilitate the acknowledgement of the lack of choices for women. Both inhibit the 'you ought' response, however covert it may be.

For example, recognising that difficulties in relationships with men are a part of many women's lives focuses attention and practice on how support can be gained from the woman's network and from other women. Where this does not already exist, intervention is focused on finding ways of providing this support through local women's groups. If necessary, it involves finding the resources to work with others in the team and community, or trying to develop these in the private and voluntary sectors. Activities and resources may focus around the key concerns of women and the infrastructures required for social and health care, such as responding to women's health needs, creating safer and less violent communities, accessing education for their children and themselves, collective care for children or adults, learning to reduce stress and relax or be more assertive, and setting up food cooperatives or credit unions to reduce the impact of poverty and high employment in local communities. Recognising that women are oppressed and are often coping without adequate personal or community resources creates a reality and authenticity in the worker's approach.

Service provision, the organisation of agencies, training and staff development do not facilitate the recognition of generic themes in relation to women who use services or to the relationship between women workers and women using services. In spite of major advances in the availability of literature and the requirement that qualified workers are able to practise in a way that is sensitive to gender, there remains a major deficiency in practice theory and the opportunities to develop practice expertise. Eight years on from the first edition of this book, the significance of gender continues to be grouped under three main headings based on women's unequal access to economic and social resources.

Women as carers

Women are defined in relation to the roles they perform for men, children and other relatives. They still have a career as carers first, as defined by Finch and Groves in 1983. Women are usually the responsible parent in one- or two-parent families. In practice, there are few expectations regarding fatherhood. Attempts to impose financial responsibilities on men for their children in first and subsequent families through the Child

Support Agency has met with substantial opposition from men because the state set limits on their rights to replace their financial responsibilities for their children and with social security.

Parenting means mothering

This is best illustrated by the extreme case, even if it is seen as bad practice within social work. Fathers, biological or social, who abuse their children may never or rarely be seen in subsequent monitoring of the children's progress by social workers. The mother will be seen and held responsible for ensuring that the children are not abused again. This is particularly acute with a black mother (DoH, 1995a). She continues sometimes to be condemned for not knowing what was going on, even though she may be in a state of shock. Even when the father is seen and worked with as a perpetrator, the emphasis is on his need to change, while with the mother the focus remains on monitoring.

Caring for adults

The care of dependent adults is still seen as primarily the responsibility of women, even though organisations like the Carers National Association urge everyone seriously to consider whether they should undertake these responsibilities. Women remain the largest group of carers and are more likely to be providing the most intimate care, to go on caring for longer and to give up employment in order to continue caring as more intensive and extensive support is required. As women tend to live longer than men, they can expect to spend a part of their later years caring for the man with whom they live. Social expectations of the level, regularity and duration of care are higher for women than for men. A son, husband or father may be condemned for not visiting regularly enough but be praised for keeping up weekly visits and doing the shopping. This is clearly not the actual behaviour of men but a reflection of social expectations that may also be held by workers. A woman in the same position is expected, and will expect of herself, much more than this before she is awarded public approbation as a 'good' wife, daughter or mother. Even though there is a theoretical understanding of how this process operates, different valuations are placed on the same behaviour, depending on the gender of the carer.

Women as subordinate to men

Caring for men has a special quality as the services that women perform are not recognised as such. Women in relation to men are seen as dependents who are cared for. The washing, cooking, cleaning, nursing, entertaining and so on that women do for men are invisible labour and remain so in spite of the fact that women in the 1990s are now key contributors to the household income. This holds true even though there is evidence that younger women are defining themselves less and less in terms of their relationship with a man or of supporting him to achieve his own goals. The lack of reciprocity is ignored or is masked by assumptions about the amount men contribute towards carrying out household tasks. There has been little change in the allocation of responsibilities over the past 10 years in spite of major continuing changes in the composition of households and in the number of working parents (Wilkinson, 1994).

Women here are not carers but social subordinates; labour is a right, a gift that cannot be recognised or counted in assessing the nature of the relationship. Failure to comply with these unrecognised labour requirements becomes a justification for maltreatment (see Chapter 5). To expose these expectations, substitute the picture of an elderly parent and son for the wife who is regrettably hit by her husband if, say, his dinner is not on the table on time. This excuse is very likely to be seen as inadequate and bizarre if offered by a son for an attack on his elderly mother, especially since the issue of elder abuse has rightly become a key concern. The recognition of differential responses by workers, such as in this example, exposes institutionalised sexism.

Women and personal identity

All approaches to working with women treat identity as crucial in overcoming specific symptoms of distress and in empowering women to use their own resources and those of others to overcome the social problems they face (Burden and Gottlieb, 1987; Phillipson, 1992; Morris, 1996). In many life experiences, women report a lack of self-esteem and feelings of worthlessness; a previously secure sense of identity can suddenly be overwhelmed by life events. Why is this? This is an aspect of women's problems that should never be ignored, even though it is now claimed that women are strongly attached to the value of autonomy and are more publicly visible and assertive.

We develop these themes in the following chapters, beginning with women's life patterns and the context in which women live.

Questions

1. What do you think you have in common with women using services? How do you think you differ from them?
2. What do you think are the most important ways in which women who use services are:
    (i)   Worse off
    (ii) Better off
    than women social workers or care staff?
3. Can you think of a social or community situation in which you feel powerful? Can you think of social or community situations in which you feel powerless? What factors contribute to these experiences?
4. What are the major advantages and disadvantages for you as a woman in your current post?
5. Think of work with a woman service user or carer.
    (i)   Does her situation differ from your own?
    (ii) How is it similar?
    (iii) Have you made these factors part of your practice?
6. Think of two black women.
    (i)   In what ways are their situations different or similar?
    (ii) Do the differences and similarities you have identified apply to you?
    Ask yourself the same questions about two disabled women and two women with mental health problems.

3

Women, Dependency and Poverty

Chapter 3 explores women's life patterns and the context in which women live in order to create a foundation for thinking about women-centred practice. It begins by explaining why it is necessary to go back to basics. Statistical data on women's lives precede a discussion of cultural assumptions about what constitutes a socially 'correct' life for women. The triangle of poverty, substandard housing and poor health experienced by many women service users provides the context for many women's lives. The central position of women in resolving these problems for families has both positive and negative implications for women.

Why rethink women's lives?

To make women-centred assessments and plans, workers need:

- To keep up to date on information about women and their life patterns, including policies that may apply to women and the services women use
- To develop an awareness of assumptions that serve to structure the assessment of individuals and groups of women
- To maintain and develop their skills and expertise in working within the changing context of women's lives.

It is rare that the relationship with a service user is one to one. The vast majority of work is with other people in the woman's social network and inside and outside our own workplace. This happens because of the way in which welfare provision and our work are organised, and because

40

many of the problems women bring are complex, having multiple rather than single causes. Intervention requires the resources of more than one person or agency. Woman-centred assessments and practice are therefore much greater than changing ourselves and our own agencies.

The question is how to begin. The frameworks underpinning social policy, practice theories and provision determine what is seen, heard and considered important, and have to be continually addressed for two reasons. The first is that women-centred practice is not static: it is changing and facing new challenges. These include:

- A reassertion of patriarchal values and structures (Faludi, 1992; Figes, 1994)
- The inadequate attention given by feminist perspectives to disabled women and women from minority ethnic groups (Ahmad, 1990; Morris, 1996)
- The fact that the most vulnerable women continue to be stigmatised and blamed for social ills for which men have a major responsibility, for example women being lone parents (Figes, 1994)
- Black and minority ethnic women continue to have issues and concerns that are underestimated by white women, although some progress has been made in mainstream provision (Butt, 1994) and through the development of specialist services by black and minority ethnic communities (Butt and Box, 1997).

The second reason is that there are contradictions in social policies that interact over time in complex ways. During the past century, social policies have hovered around recognising how the impact of poverty, illness and disadvantage limit people's ability to parent and provide care. A fear persists of provoking dependence and raising expectations, and of social dislocation and disorder, if old imperatives and responsibilities are rapidly changed. Leading up to the beginning of the twenty-first century, individuals and families are expected to take greater responsibility for their own social care, which is balanced by an emphasis on the state working in partnership with citizens.

Evidence is accumulating on the centrality of women in improving the health and education of children, and on the detrimental effects of domestic violence on both those who witness it and those who experience it (Heise and Germain, 1994). While more women than men provide personal support to other adults, they are not recognised as a legitimate grouping in social work or social care. There are no statutory responsibilities to women as a group as there are, for example, for children and older people. When a child or older person is abused, workers are required by statute to act. With abused women, decisions are of a different order. The worker who acts in such cases may be deemed culpable of undue haste or of breaking up a marriage. Domestic violence is being prioritised not because of the impact on women but because of a link to the abuse of children (DoH, 1995a) and because of long-term effects on the emotional, educational and physical development of children (Saunders, 1995).

Responses are socially constructed in a way that creates difficulties in learning about women and applying knowledge about women in conscious ways. Knowledge about women is not structured to make it easier to use. Basic qualifying programmes (CCETSW, 1995; S/NVQ, 1997) support teaching on gender, but the move from rhetoric to how to apply new ways of working does not always happen. Gender may still be largely banished from practice teaching into the territories of the contributory disciplines of psychology, sociology and social policy. There is learning about women but much less on the practice and provision that supports women.

Women's life patterns

If we look at women's lives over the life cycle, we see that women experience more than one pattern of living. Women often begin life in a one- or two-parent nuclear family. They may marry or cohabit directly from their family of origin or after a short time of living alone or in some more collective setting with other women and men. The marriage is more likely to result in children than not, and many women spend some time as a single parent or again as a single person. Most divorced women remarry, although a significant proportion do not. Finally, at the end of her life, a woman may spend a few years alone again or with other adults to whom she may or may not be related. Married women, like single women or married men, may have relationships with their own or the opposite sex while remaining married.

These patterns are not 'abnormal' or even undesirable in and of themselves. It is the social valuation and expectations that we place on people that result in negative value judgements. The actual lives of women are deviating more and more from the cultural ideal of lifelong marriage with inevitable motherhood and parenting by both biological parents. These points are relevant when making assessments as a variety of patterns of living, on either a permanent or a temporary basis, are experienced by an increasing number of people. Trends particularly relevant for workers to consider are:

- An increasing number of couples have a period of living together before they marry: 60 per cent in 1992 compared with 6 per cent in 1971. Most people in their late twenties have lived together, compared with 1 in 10 of the over sixties (Utting, 1995). Marriage is both being postponed and has decreased to the lowest point since records began, while the number of cohabiting couples has doubled since the 1970s.
- Women are tending to have their children later. The mean age for the birth of the first child is 28 years, compared with 24 years in 1992. For the mothers of children born outside marriage, the mean age is younger: 20–24 years. One-fifth of mothers are under 20 years of age. One of the diversities between women is that those who are poor and unemployed are likely to have their children at a younger age than those in well-paid employment (Utting, 1995).
- It is estimated that one-fifth of women born between the 1960s and 90s will remain childless (Wilkinson and Mulgan, 1995), although this prediction has to stand the test of time given that women now have children later.
- Although the majority – 72 per cent – of children grow up with their birth parents, and 7 per cent live in step-families, a substantial minority – 21 per cent – are living in one-parent families. The vast majority of these, about 91 per cent, are headed by women. The proportion of families headed by men has remained at about 9 per cent. In the past 20 years, the proportion of children growing up in a one-parent family has risen from 1 in 12 to 1 in 5 (Utting, 1995). The statistics on one-parent families do not fully incorporate the number of women who have spent a shorter or longer time caring for children on their own either because of ending a relationship with a man or because he is employed from home or in another country.
- The 1991 Census reports an increasing number of one-parent families in the white community, with a similar proportion in the Bangladeshi and Pakistani communities. One-parent families are most common in the black community and least common among Indian families: 40 per cent of black children live in one-parent families, as do 10 per cent of Asian children. About 1 in 5 minority ethnic 5-year-olds is of mixed ethnicity (Coleman and Salt, 1996).
- The average lone parent has one child and is a woman of 34 years who

has been married or has cohabited for a long period. Younger women find a second partner more quickly than older women, single parenthood lasting an average of 4 years. The estimate is that if present trends continue, 2 out of 5 children will spend some time within a single-parent household by the year 2020 (Utting, 1995).

- In 1992, 215,000 babies were born outside marriage and 19 per cent were born to mothers under 20 years old. While young people who have children outside marriage have received very negative comments from individual government Ministers and MPs during the 1990s, their number is relatively small and continues to decrease (Utting, 1995). Only 1 in 10 single mothers were under 20 years of age in 1996. The number of births to teenage mothers is actually smaller than it was in the 1970s and is falling again after a temporary increase.

- A growing number of older women are having children. Since 1971, there has been a 33 per cent increase in the number of women having children in their forties, and there are now more women in their thirties giving birth than in younger age groups (Wilkinson and Mulgan, 1995).

- Three out of 10 babies are born to unmarried women, compared with 1 out of 17 in the 1960s. About half of these are registered by both parents (Utting, 1995).

- The greatest proportion of single-parent families arises as the result of divorce, with 4 in 10 new marriages expected to end in divorce (Wilkinson and Mulgan, 1995). An increasing number of men and women experience serial monogamy, that is marriage, divorce and remarriage. Remarriage accounted for 1 in 5 marriages in the 1970s and 1 in 3 in 1992 (Utting, 1995).

- There is a reduction in the number of people occupying households. Twenty-six per cent of households are occupied by one person with no other family, while only 29 per cent of households have children under 16 years of age. Older women over 75 years old are more likely to live alone or outside a family context (Utting, 1995).

- An increasing number of married women with children are in employment. Three out of 5 married women are in jobs in the early 1990s compared with 1 out of 4 in the 1970s. If pensioners are excluded, 7 out of 10 married women are in employment. Fifty-nine per cent of women with dependent children are in jobs in the 1990s compared with 49 per cent in the 1970s, and another 6 per cent are actively looking for employment. Women are returning to work earlier after the birth of a child. In 1992, 1 in 2 women with children under 5 years old was in the workforce compared with 1 in 4 during the 1970s. The majority of women with children under 5 years are working part time (Utting, 1995).

- Employment patterns have changed so greatly that 3 out of 10 children aged 2 and under live in a family with both parents in employment. The majority of secondary school children have both parents in employment. The growing number of dual-income families has reduced the number of families living in poverty.

- The gulf between the incomes of single parents and the growing number of dual-parent households is widening. Single parents are at 'greater risk of poverty than their predecessors 20 years ago when little more than one third were receiving supplementary benefit' (Utting, 1995, p. 27), as income support was then called. In the UK, a lower proportion of lone mothers is in employment than in the 20 countries surveyed by Bradshaw and his colleagues, and we have the lowest proportion in full-time employment (1996). Lone parenthood for women means dependence on state benefits.

- Forty-two per cent of lone parents held jobs between 1981 and 1992 (Utting, 1995). Welfare to work policies, family credit and assistance with day care costs are increasing this number. Many women heading up one-parent families want to work and to remove themselves from the benefit system, but the main disincentive is child care costs compared with those in the other countries (Bradshaw *et al.*, 1996).

- Poverty is not limited to unemployed or poorly paid woman-headed families. It is estimated that the number of households where neither adult partner is working has increased from 6 per cent in 1979 to 20 per cent in 1996.

- An overt challenge to heterosexuality as the only valid form of sexual relationship and way of life is continuing (Rich, 1980). We do not know the statistical significance of this, but many women are more open about their relationships with other women, given a slightly more positive social climate than in the past. A figure of 1 in 10 is often cited as the proportion of women who have made a primary attachment to women rather than men (Rights of Women Lesbian Custody Group, 1986). A few women choose to live with other women in preference to living with men or alone. This is viewed more negatively than any other lifestyle, yet women do live with each other, often in preference to any other way of life. Women raise children together, often with great success, but the fear of social censure and of legal and social work intervention may necessitate careful presentation or a denial of these living arrangements.

- An increasing number of women live without men because women live longer than men. In the 75–84 year age group, 6 out of 10 are women, and of those 85 and older, 7 out of 10 are women (Levin and Moriarty, 1994). Many women live alone at the end of their lives. Living alone is something that is supposed to happen only at the end of one's life and then inadvertently; living alone is believed to be a poor second to marriage. One of Sophie Tucker's songs, *I'm Living Alone and I Like It*, expresses a deviant point of view. Women are not supposed to like it, but we all know of exceptions. For example, one of us had a grandmother who never looked back once her husband died: a much more fulfilling life of paid employment and social independence opened up for her.

- Although they constitute a small proportion statistically, a number of women never marry. Unmarried women enjoy better mental health than those who marry, but they may be expected to give up employment to look after ageing parents or other relations. Living alone does not mean that women are free from domestic responsibilities towards others.

A socially correct life

Irrespective of the actual lives of women, there are commonly accepted organising principles governing views on the happiness and social correctness of women's lives. These principles apply to women across ethnic groups and embody value judgements in relation to:

- Whether or not women are living with men
- Whether or not women have children
- Whether or not women take appropriate responsibilities for dependent relatives.

To choose consciously to not live with men, to not have children and to not care for dependent relatives is seen as deviant behaviour. These outcomes are not as easily available for women from all ethnic and religious groups living in Britain, but the principles governing women's lives are the same. Deviant behaviours are ranked in order of importance. Not to live with men is the greatest deviance, followed by not having children, while the least deviant is not caring for dependent relatives. Among more recent migrants, particularly from the Indian subcontinent, these three requirements governing the lives of women are closely interrelated, particularly when women are living in extended households.

In the dominant culture, an inability to achieve either marriage or children when these are seen to be desired and sought by the woman is more likely to result in sympathy from family, friends, neighbours and society generally, although it can lead to divorce and remarriage for the man. Conscious deviance, however, can result in censure and efforts to recall the woman to the 'correct way of life'.

Increasing emphasis is being placed on the importance of having a male partner where there are male children to rear as men are deemed to be a source of control and an adult role model. Lack of a male is frequently seen as the reason boys become out of control, and as a failure on the part of the woman as mother to ensure the correct environment for growth to mature malehood. When women are expected to find their own husband, the lack of a boyfriend or marriage plans can lead to expressions of related concerns and even efforts to effect introductions, and to a direct questioning of intentions. This is not an issue among groups where marriages are arranged; in Britain, this is the dominant form among Muslims, Sikhs and Hindus. Among ethnic groups where boys are more valued than girls, having children, if they are girls, may not be sufficient.

These ideological responses to, and demands on, women can be experienced as devastatingly oppressive and restrictive. Even for women who want nothing more than to meet these demands, however, the struggle to achieve and maintain a 'socially correct life' is made particularly difficult by family and community poverty. Many women who use social service provision live in these conditions.

These life patterns create and are based on women's financial dependency on men and the state. In the 1980s, financial needs and housing issues were the problems most often brought to social workers by women, and these continue to dominate in the 1990s. The economic context in which women who use services live is that of poverty interlinked with inadequate housing and poor health. This triangle of conditions forms the backdrop of women's lives whichever agency they come into contact with – social services, community groups, probation, voluntary or private agencies.

What is poverty?

- Women comprise 50 per cent of the global population.
- Women make up one-third of the paid labour force.
- Women work two-thirds of all working hours.

- Women receive one-tenth of the world's income.
- Women own less than 1 per cent of the world's property.

Before we explore the poverty women live with and amidst, we must consider what we mean by poverty. The way in which we conceive of poverty will influence not only how we attempt to measure and alleviate it, but also its very nature and the way we think it is experienced. Definitions of poverty have varied over time. Rowntree, in the late nineteenth century, took as his base what was required to ensure 'merely physical efficiency' – that which was necessary for human survival. Adequate clothing for a young woman was 'one pair of boots, two aprons, one second hand dress, one skirt made from an old dress, a third of the cost of a new hat, a third of the cost of a shawl, and a jacket, two pairs of stockings, a few unspecified underclothes, one pair of stays and one pair of old boots worn as slippers' (Townsend, 1979, p. 50).

Today, poverty is viewed in relation to a generally accepted standard of living that goes beyond basic physical needs and material well-being. When assessing poverty, we must also include our social well-being because our needs are socially constructed and are not solely physical and material. People in poverty, are those 'deprived of the conditions of life which ordinarily define membership of society' (Townsend, 1979, p. 915). People must have enough income and command over resources to enable participation in the life of the community. What is hotly debated is which conditions should be measured and what constitutes a minimum standard of living. Townsend's 'relative deprivation' definition of poverty included food, clothing, utilities, employment, health, schooling, neighbourhood, leisure and social life. The study considered the quality of life as well as physical survival and income.

All too often, it is the women parenting without a man who is seen as the problem. As poverty is one of the main reasons for contact with social services agencies, it is inevitable that lone parents – mainly women – will be particularly vulnerable to needing or being required to become a user of social services. The chances of a child or young person coming into care is directly related to income. For example, a report from the Department of Health in 1991 (DoH, 1991) found that for children aged 5–9 years in families living on income support, there was a 1 in 10 chance of being admitted into care. The risk was drastically reduced – 1 in 7000 – for the same age group in families not on income support.

Women struggle to reduce the vulnerability that poverty brings their children. Elaine Kempson (1996) found that there were highly developed money management skills among people living on benefits. These they often learnt as children, particularly from their mothers. Women bear the brunt and the strain of managing on low incomes whether they are living with men, are lone mothers or are pensioners. The difficulties are compounded for women or their families who needed special diets for health reasons. Women use numerous strategies to cope, such as shopping daily so that the intake of food is limited and hence spread more evenly throughout the week, putting aside money regularly to pay the different bills, shopping around, going without food themselves and making sure that children do not stand out at school by getting the right clothes and shoes. These are the historical strategies used by women, ones reminiscent of our own childhood.

It is particularly ironic, given these heroic efforts, that women are often blamed for their own poverty, even though economic and political trends have increased the number of families with children living in poverty. These include, at the macro level, changes in the labour market, housing policies that increasingly concentrate lone parents into particular neighbourhoods and estates, and the shift to indirect as opposed to direct taxation. In day-to-day living, women are having to cope with the loss of local shops and markets, where fruit and vegetables are often cheaper, and with their replacement by supermarkets, often at a distance from their homes (Low Income Project Team for the Nutrition Task Force, 1996). The decline in public transport impacts on access to increasingly centralised health care and benefits offices. It is probably no coincidence that one-third of families are living in poverty and that one-third of households do not have cars. Policies that focus on public health and community regeneration recognise that surviving in poverty becomes more difficult when the infrastructure to support social well-being is fragmented or undermined.

Households headed by women have over the centuries been blamed for the social behaviour of their children. A causal link is made between the lone woman parent and any deviance on the part of her children. For young men, this is usually their public behaviour, violence, disruption and criminal behaviour, and for young women their sexual behaviour. The absence of a clear male role model, either because of male absence or because of the mother's relationship with a number of men, is seen to result in a failure to provide adequate control both in the home and outside it. It is true that one of the risk factors for youth crime is divorce in families, but this is only one of a number of factors. Others include low income and poor housing, living in an inner city area, parental conflict, poor supervision and low school attainment. Young black males are at a

much higher risk of being stopped by the police and are disproportionately represented in the criminal justice system. This places black and
minority ethnic lone mothers under greater pressure, which is likely to
make them fear contact with social service agencies.

Sources of poverty

To speak of poverty is to speak of inequality. The sources of inequality
are usually defined in terms of class, gender, race and disability. These
factors interact. Poverty is widely associated with social class, but in
recent years, greater attention has been given to examining discrimination based on gender, race, disability and age.

The phrase 'feminisation of poverty' describes women's position so
that, whether employed or unemployed, the majority of women cannot get
out of poverty or escape the danger of being catapulted into it. Many
women are dependent on the income of the man they live with for their
class status, and lose their position and their lifestyle when their relationship ends. Women in employment are often kept poor because of their low
wages, and the number of one-parent families in the UK, which are mostly
headed by women, are especially vulnerable to poverty (Ford *et al.*, 1998).

Race, too, is a significant source of inequality and poverty. As in the
1980s, black and minority ethnic groups still experience disadvantages
because of unemployment, overcrowding, households lacking the
exclusive use of amenities and lower pension rights. Many of the same
afflictions are shared by poor whites, but what divides black and white
experience is racism. Whether we are looking at housing, environment
or day care for the under 5s, it is clear that, although it is not their
exclusive preserve, ethnic minorities experience poverty and its
accompanying conditions in greater degrees than does the white population. Environmental poverty and racism can be forgotten in our concentration on individual women as 'fit' mothers or when supporting adults.
Understanding the wider meaning of poverty is crucial, and it is to this
that we now turn.

Poverty and disability

Disabled people have fewer opportunities for employment than non-
disabled people. As a result they are vulnerable to poverty, to living on

benefits and to poor pension rights. This inevitably impacts on the quality of housing and the level and nature of support they can secure to live independently. Poverty for disabled women means that their homes can become their only environment because they are forced to be housebound. The non-disabled poor experience problems similar to those seen with discrimination based on race, but for disabled women these are compounded. The introduction of Direct Payments in 1996, together with policies that address access to transport, public buildings and employment, can be undermined unless the changes are sufficient to make a difference. Poverty also impacts on disabled children and their families since access to a car gives easier access to resources in the community and to education, training and employment (Morris, 1996).

The dimensions of poverty

Poverty affects all aspects of life. It is about not having access to basic material goods and services, but it is also about living in a run-down environment with no resources and with no space to dream. It is about how these things compound and interact with one another. For women, this interaction of factors is pervasive because the home is their industrial workplace. Women labour in the home, often in substandard conditions, and constantly have to deal with the problem of 'doing without'.

The experience of poverty has a profound effect on women's lives and on their children and the adults they support. In a conversation about race and class as interacting oppressions, Beverly Smith commented:

> When I think of poverty, I think of constant physical and material oppression. You know, you aren't poor one day and well-to-do the next. If you're poor it's a constant thing, everyday, everyday. In some ways it's almost more constant than race because, say you're middle class and you're a black person who is of course subject to racism, you don't necessarily experience it every single day in the same intensity, or to the same degree. (Smith and Smith, 1981, p. 115)

So being poor is not simply about doing without things. It is also about experiencing poor health, isolation, stress, stigma and exclusion, and about feeling powerless. Women are especially vulnerable to all these dimensions of poverty and more. We have already seen how poverty and a dependence on benefits increases the vulnerability of children to being in the public care. These pressures are greater for families from black and minority ethnic groups because of their higher incidence of poverty.

Racism and environmental factors locate the statistics on black children in care in a broader context. This improves our understanding of why black children are more likely to be accommodated in care and enables a question to be raised about the appropriateness of this remedy.

Living in poverty demands greater physical and psychological effort and stamina from women who take on family-based caring responsibilities. By not interpreting the unpaid work women do as work, it is possible to ignore the skills and needs of women in a way that is not possible in paid work. The connection between the task expected of the worker and the economic means of carrying it out is obscured for all but the woman herself. She stands alone with this knowledge and her difficult-to-impossible work environment. Shifting the burden onto individual women in this way creates physical, mental and emotional stress for women as workers.

The stress in the struggle to survive poverty is well illustrated by one task expected of women: making and maintaining connections with numerous different agencies. The lack of material resources for day-to-day living means that the poor are often in continuous contact with the Benefits Agency, the gas, electricity and water agencies, and housing departments. These are separate entities. But the effect of having to decide whether to use money for heating or for food has a direct impact on their housing conditions – housing stock can deteriorate because of damp – and health. These will in turn have an effect on the demands made on health and social services.

Poverty may also bring with it educational problems for children. Poverty often compounds educational disadvantages for black and disabled children by channelling them into particular jobs and labelling them as troublemakers or difficult because they are different. Black and minority ethnic communities in the late 1990s still find it necessary to have a system of Saturday schools to combat racism in the education system and to maintain their cultural identity. Some progress has been made since the 1960s in the acceptance of Afro-Caribbean and Asian cultures and languages, but this does not mean that the people themselves have been accepted (Adebowale, 1998). Racism means that black mothers must intervene and negotiate on behalf of their children in the education system. While white mothers, in particular working-class mothers, also undertake these tasks, black mothers have the additional dimension of racism to contend with.

Families where there are children with impairment are more likely to be poor than are those with non-disabled children. In addition, children also still experience discrimination and can be excluded from mainstream education because of poor access to buildings as well as concerns about any additional demands on time and the organisation of the school day. While policies now encourage placing disabled children and children with learning difficulties in mainstream education, in practice this position often has to be fought for. Mothers struggling with poverty can lack the space to take on these battles for their children or to sustain them long enough to succeed.

It is women who negotiate with the organisations that control the resources they need for daily living, just as it is women who present themselves at social services with their families' problems. Women undertake these negotiations even when they are employed or when the men with whom they live are unemployed. Carrying responsibility for making and maintaining connections with agencies – what we call networking – is often accepted without question as the woman's job; it is an integral component of her role as carer. Workers are well aware that this work is time-consuming even with access to telephones and cars. People using services often are without these resources.

Housing

Poor, inadequate housing and homelessness are the consequences of poverty. Poor-quality social and private rented housing is occupied by the most disadvantaged women, men and children in our society. To be poor is to have insufficient money to buy or rent spacious, good-quality housing in 'good' neighbourhoods, but, additionally, the quality of housing, particularly social housing, varies regionally. Some areas have sufficient housing stock, but a substantial proportion will be in bad condition, and it is in this type of housing that the poorest live. Where there is sufficient housing stock, there may not be employment opportunities. Other areas, particularly London and the surrounding districts, offer better employment prospects but have a major housing deficit.

Black people often live in conditions significantly worse than those of the general population (Butt and Mirza, 1996). In addition, they may suffer harassment from neighbours. Although some local authorities and housing associations are actively taking steps to change this situation, it can mean that black families are concentrated on certain estates, whose houses may be in worse condition than many other properties.

Women's housing prospects are closely tied to their family status and ideals of domesticity and family life. Women without men have limited access to owner occupation because of their low incomes and attitudes towards the commitment and capacity of women to remain in the labour market. Women, and poor women especially, are heavily reliant on public sector housing policies, and these are powerful conditioning factors in their lives.

The increase in marriage breakdown means that many women are faced with the issue of finding independent access to housing. Marital break-up can lead to poverty. Women can get caught in a downward spiral of high mortgage payments, arrears and ultimately homelessness. These housing stresses are especially severe for women forced out of their homes by violence. Women's Aid, with its network of refugees, highlights the connections between poverty, housing and health.

The economic and family relationships on which housing finance and allocation are based marginalise one-parent families. The housing tenure of single parents is a clear indication of their disadvantage and difference from other families (Utting, 1995). They are far less likely to be owner-occupiers, are more dependent on social housing and are particularly concentrated in private furnished accommodation. The private sector contains the worst of all housing conditions and is the most expensive. Thus one-parent families often live in poor and insecure accommodation at a high cost that takes up a higher proportion of their income than is the case for better-off families.

Social housing remains the main recourse for those women who have a high risk of becoming homeless. Where there is no access to social housing, women often find themselves in temporary accommodation. There is a danger that the numerous young women with young children in bed and breakfast accommodation in inner city areas will be forgotten or will, by sleight of hand, be excluded from our thinking about housing problems. Although their living conditions are slightly better than the night shelters in which increasing numbers of people are sleeping, the stress on women and their children who may remain in unsuitable temporary accommodation, often for months, is enormous.

The single homeless woman suffers not only from the shortage of accommodation that confronts all single homeless people, but also from services that incompletely recognise her gender-related needs. The traditional image of homeless single people tends to be male. Because fewer women are to be seen sleeping rough, there is an assumption that fewer women than men become homeless. Rarely do we stop to question this or to find out whether there are really fewer homeless women around or whether women adopt different solutions to their housing problems or homelessness. *The Big Issue*, the weekly newspaper produced by homeless people, has consistently brought the plight of homeless women, including their vulnerability to sexual assault, to the fore. When homelessness is combined with mental health problems, it heightens the likelihood that the women will not be believed and that no action will be taken to protect them.

Health

The triangle of poverty and substandard housing is completed by poor health. This is a major concern for many of the women using services. Their concerns range from the debilitating effects of parenting disabled children to drug and alcohol abuse. The term 'depression' recurs, even when they are older and in residential care (Schneider *et al.*, 1997).

Women's health problems relate to their role as carers of men, children and dependent adults in a context of poverty. In particular, the guilt experienced by women who are too ill or disabled to go on with cleaning, cooking and caring for their families is seen by some as a personal and gendered failure for women, one that makes them feel unfeminine. In the 1990s, the level of income on which many women have to manage is too low to meet the health needs of the women and their families (Kempson, 1996).

When the main problem is seen as the inability to budget rather than the inadequacy of the benefit level, it is largely women who are criticised and held responsible for the harm that this does to others. Yet women often reduce their personal consumption to aid the collective consumption of their family. In other words, they are the first to feel the effects of any economies. Such strategies are highly apparent among unemployed women. Cutting back on food and heating for the entire family are the areas most amenable to further economy. Women are forced to make choices between health-keeping and housekeeping. The consequences of budget deficits for health are particularly marked for the very young and the very old, that is, those for whom women care. In the late 1990s, healthy eating is part of policies underpinning the Health of the Nation strategy. Women living in poverty are often accused of failing to provide healthy food for their children. The fallacies of this position are well exposed by Elaine Kempson (1996) in her work on living on benefits.

The effect of these coping strategies on women's health is both hidden and unknown. There is a considerable literature dating back to the 1970s on the effects of unemployment on men's health (Hill, 1977), but much less attention has been paid to how unemployment affects women's health. The unemployment of a husband or cohabitee influences not only the man's health, but also that of the woman and the children with whom he lives. Women also often give up a job, or give up looking for one, when a man becomes unemployed because of the effect that her employment will have on the family's benefits. She is then left to cope on a dramatically reduced income, with an increased likelihood of illness among her children and with her own personal reactions, as well as those of the man with whom she is living, to unemployment.

Transport

Access to transport is another important resource that tends to be ignored when examining dimensions of inequality and poverty. Car ownership is directly related to social class and gender. When a car is available, men usually have priority use of it; women have to walk or rely on public transport. Indeed, the majority of all bus passengers are women (*Social Trends*, 1998).

With the reduction in bus services and the increases in fares in recent years, options for women on low income to get out of the home and off the estates or out of the areas in which they live are diminishing. As women are mainly responsible for liaising with agencies, the decrease in services means they have to struggle harder to reach the resources necessary for their families' well-being, such as doctors, health centres, benefit offices, food and other shops, and play facilities. Women in rural areas and on large housing estates are particularly adversely affected. These problems of access show how far we are from realising the principle of organising key services within 'pram-pushing distance' (Richards, 1987). There is an immense backlog for planners aiming to reverse these trends in line with policies on community regeneration and accessible environments. Older people who use services and carers are most likely to be isolated without transport enabling them to access community-based resources, including user- or carer-controlled provision and support.

Access to transport is one means of increasing personal safety for women. During the 5-year period when the mass murderer of women, the so-called 'Yorkshire Ripper', roamed the north of England, women showed their understanding of transport as a means of improving their safety. Women who usually walked acquired bicycles, those who usually cycled moved onto buses and so on. Black women face the same dangers as white women as well as the likelihood of more frequent racial and sexual attacks.

Poverty for women not only entails a low income and struggles from day to day to make ends meet in poor physical surroundings, but also contributes to a worsening of mental and physical health along with a major reduction in options and opportunities generally. However, women are not the passive victims of poverty. As we have seen, they use their skills to manage and overcome it. They look to whatever resources are available to them in this struggle. One of these resources is employment.

The central position of women

Economic restructuring is reducing the proportion of state spending available for health and social well-being in the UK, Europe and globally, and the resulting change in the labour market can influence gender relations. We have already looked at the increasing number of married women in employment and the fact that they are returning to work earlier after the birth of each child. In the labour market as a whole in the UK, the main growth in jobs has been in part-time work in areas traditionally seen as 'women's work', with full-time jobs declining in number. Men are 6 per cent more likely to be unemployed than are women in Britain. The wage gap between women and men increases with age. Four-fifths of 33-year-old women living with a man were earning substantially less than half his wages, and few in this generation will match their husbands' pensions (Joshi *et al.*, 1995), whereas for younger women aged 16–24, the wage gap has been narrowed to 4.3 per cent compared with 50 per cent for 35–55-year-olds (Wilkinson and Mulgan, 1995).

Women in employment with qualifications and career plans are seen as setting the pace and as having greater self-esteem and confidence than either their contemporaries without employment or the older generation of women. The changes are marked in relation to the number of women entering medicine, dentistry and the law. It is expected that professional jobs will be the highest growth area for women in the future. At present, women hold 38 per cent of professional jobs (Wilkinson, 1994). This creates a difference between the women in social service agencies who are professionally qualified and those who have had little access to opportunities for qualification, many of whom will be in low-paid employment in residential and home care. Access to income and a higher degree of job security than either colleagues or service users gives women social workers the potential for greater control over their own lives and hence more power in their relationships with men. It also brings certain risks. Women in senior management are more likely to be single or divorced than are their male counterparts; this also holds true in social services departments (Balloch *et al.*, 1995). Relationships with men can be fraught where there is the expectation that the woman with a career will service the man, children and home at the same time as the job.

It is not possible to take one form of family life, that is, one-parent families, and correlate this directly to particular outcomes, because there are complex relationships between factors influencing the behaviour and achievements of young people. Strategies to overcome multiple social handicaps relate not to family composition but to support for parents, day care, nursery education and training children to stop and think (Farrington, 1996). Social work and social care strategies that are woman centred will address the whole range of the dynamics affecting women parenting on their own, even though much will be out of the control or remedy of social service agencies.

Women occupy a central position in the resolution of these problems. Investment in women is seen as one of the main means of improving the health and educational attainment of children (World Bank, 1993). The role that women have in tackling problems ranging from poverty, poor health and low educational attainment, to social exclusion and male violence is something the feminists have identified over many years. Its new visibility has both positive and negative consequences for women. The analysis that has placed women in this key position has different and conflicting bases. This may be because the forces themselves are impacting on women differently, by age and their position in the labour market for example.

Elaine Kempson (1996), in her study of life on a low income, found that conceptions of masculinity were still strongly linked to being the breadwinner, with the consequence that an inability of provide because of unemployment or low wages could lead to conflict. Women were attached less strongly to the labour market and more to motherhood. In contrast, Wilkinson and Mulgan (1995) found among younger people a more androgynous view of gender roles, a greater attachment among women with career prospects to the labour market and a much lower attachment to motherhood as a source of fulfilment. Seen in a positive light, this presents a major challenge to social service agencies in the UK to recognise the significance of gender in their provision and practice, and in the patterning of male–female and female–female relationships. A less hopeful view is that women will become the focus of increasing pressure as a resource to resolve the social impact of economic and demographic change.

The next chapter will examine the demands associated with social expectations for those born female.

Questions

1. Think of the women who you have worked with or know. How is poverty affecting their lives?
2. Are the black or minority ethnic families who you work with or know financially worse off than the white families? If they are, what effect is this having on the lives of Afro-Caribbean, Asian and other minority ethnic women?
3. Are agencies more responsive to the needs of one-parent families headed by men than by women? What factors do you think influence this outcome?
4. What are the major housing issues for the women with whom you work? Are some women more adversely affected than others? How would you explain these differences?
5. Do you think that the physical and mental problems of the women with whom you work are related to their role as carers of men, children and dependent adults in a context of poverty? If not, what other factors are particularly important?

4

Women and Care for Children and Adults

The separation of children and adults into different service divisions makes little sense to women who undertake care for many people over a lifetime. This chapter begins by introducing why providing care is increasingly a women's issue. It then looks at types of care, children and assessments of 'fit mothering', and the problem of involuntary childlessness. Caring for adult relatives then follows.

Why providing care is increasingly a woman's issue

Community and child care legislation places the responsibility for personal care firmly on the immediate family and relatives. This is in spite of legislative recognition that carers have needs of their own and that these may conflict with those of the person needing support. What is called an 'inverse care law' operates, which means that people with access to informal carers are less likely to receive support (Harding *et al.*, 1996). While social policy for both children and adults talks about the assessment of need, the reality is that, for people who are dependent on state-funded resources, the criteria to determine eligibility are becoming ever more tightly defined. In effect, eligibility criteria are a means of reaching decisions about how to manage the budget (Pitkeathley, 1995). It is ironic that policies that originated from a government review intended to build on strengths and abilities (Griffiths, 1988) have in practice meant an increased pathologising of service uses and carers (Platt, 1996).

To receive a package of care requires those in need of support to demonstrate their weaknesses and frailties. Most families receive little or nothing from state-funded sources, and family-based care is at the centre of the care of both children and adults. Formal care provided through the different sectors is, and always has been, marginal to this (Smale, 1996). Debates about the cost of long-term care for older people can easily distort recognition of the importance of support provided through the extended family. In 1980, grandmothers were the main source of day care for children whose mothers were in full-time employment, and fathers, followed by grandmothers, were the main carers where women worked part time. The rapid increase in women's employment has not altered this pattern. By 1990, one-half of children's day care is provided by relatives, friends or neighbours, the majority of whom are women (Utting, 1995).

When combined with the demographic trend towards an ageing population, the impact of these social policies has a profound effect on women who have a career as carers. About 80 per cent of elderly people with dementia, many of whom are as frail and vulnerable as those in care and nursing homes, are cared for in the family home (Alzheimer's Disease Society, 1994). Care through the family is an important means of containing the costs to the central and local state (Schneider *et al.*, 1993). Using the term 'carer' is, as we discussed earlier, one of the ways in which women are made invisible in the social care system. Research in the 1980s confirmed that most care is carried out by women (Finch and Groves, 1983; Ungerson, 1985). This has not changed over the past decade and does not deny the contribution of men, especially the spouses of older people who need support (Levin and Moriarty, 1994). Informal carers of adults number between six and eight million in Great Britain (OPCS, 1992). Women do not just look after children: a substantial number can expect to look after a dependent adult in their middle years and early old age. Single women may also experience the role of carer. They are more likely than men to be called upon to look after either related children or other adults. Caring means work, even if it is carried out with love.

The recognition in the early 1980s that employment and caring are constantly in tension affects more women in the late twentieth century, when 59 per cent of women with dependent children are employed. When both parents are in employment, the mother whether she is working full or part time, is the one who takes time off when children are ill. Levels of satisfaction were gender related. Among women in employment, dissatisfaction was highest among those whose husbands were uninvolved with child care, and for men the highest proportion of those dissatisfied with their lives (16 per cent) lay among those most involved with their children (Ferri and Smith, 1996).

When considering the care of children and adults, the issue of income and wealth is central. More and more people are being charged for state-funded provision. As a result, provision is sometimes gone without, or one service requiring payment is prioritised over another, given an inability to meet the charges (Chetwyn *et al.*, 1996). Smale *et al.* (1994) point out that being older or a child is not a social problem, but being without access to dependable resources is. They give the example of the Queen Mother never needing to ask for an assessment from her local authority because she, and her family, have access to the resources to create and maintain an adequate support structure. Buying care and personal assistance for both children and adults directly from private service providers without the intervention of social services is becoming more common, but it is not an option for the majority of women who use social services because they are poor.

The theme of caring is crucial for women, whether they are users of services or workers in them. This is particularly so for women who are looking after children or adults requiring intensive support. This issue has been particularly prominent for disabled women and within the young carers debate. The estimate of the number of young people under the age of 16 who provide 'care' for disabled parents ranges from 10,000 to 20,000. Young carers do not usually see themselves as parenting their parents – role reversal. This construction fails to see what is actually happening in families and ignores the real problems. A different outcome is achieved if the framework for analysis employs the needs for support by the parent and the child's right to unimpeded educational and social opportunities (Keith and Morris, 1996).

Lois Keith and Jenny Morris argue that feminists have failed to address the way in which the focus on the carer's responsibility contributes to ignoring the needs of the cared for. The construction of dependence and being 'cared for' faced by disabled mothers may be encountered by other women in their later years. Women are the majority of people in the over-85 years of age group, and older women over 75 years old are most likely to live either alone or outside the family (Utting, 1995). As disability and poor health increase with age, a significant number of women move from their careers as carers into requiring some form of support in their later years. Diversity in the needs of carers and women requiring support can create conflicts and differences between women at different points in their lives.

Living with children

Households with children are now in the minority, but most women have children. This is a commonality between women, but a variation in income and qualifications is creating differences between women in their relationship to children. Women with educational qualifications and in well-paid employment are delaying childbearing, while women with little expectation of well-paid employment are having their children in their early twenties (Wilkinson and Mulgan, 1995). Both men and women without qualifications are increasingly penalised in the labour market as the demand for unskilled labour falls (Dilnot, 1996). It is this latter group of women who are the main social services users. Many workers share the experience of being a mother with those using services. Living with and caring for men, and producing, living with and caring for children, are held to be basic to a woman's life. It is a state towards which many women strive, although for some this may be less central than in the past (Wilkinson, 1994). As with living with men, the experiences we have of motherhood range from the very positive to the very negative.

Women carry the main burden of child care. This does not substantially alter even if the woman is employed or the man is unemployed, although there may be some reallocation of chores. The old adage 'men work from sun to sun and women's work is never done' illustrates the work demands on women. Child care is largely carried out in the socially isolating conditions of the one- or two-adult family household unit. The social isolation of women caring for children is a recurring theme raised by practitioners. The classic work of George Brown and Tirrell Harris into clinical depression in women with small children identified a lack of interaction at a deep personal level with another, that is, social isolation, as one of its major indicators (1978). Clinical depression is, however, a greater problem for poorer women than for those whose social isolation has the possibility of being lessened by the possession of more material resources and access to leisure. The economic context of motherhood is thus significant, and depression is one of the many adverse effects on mothers and children associated with family poverty and a poverty of resources in the local community.

Adrienne Rich, in *Of Women Born* (1977), explores the context in which women must rear children. In a deeply humane account of her own experience, she describes the conflicts between her desire and need for her three sons and the need to continue writing as a poet. This life-affirming account names the conditions of reproduction, the institution of motherhood itself, as the cause of her anguish. Rich identifies the elements of the institution of motherhood as being legal, economic, cultural and psychological. Alice Walker (1984) gives an account from a black woman's perspective that explores similar themes.

To locate the problem of mothering solely in the social isolation of mothers, or in the separation of mothers from their children, neatly side-steps a closer look at the complex interpenetration of the strands that make up the institution of motherhood as a whole. The problems become personalised. The woman's behaviour is seen as inappropriate. She is deemed unable to make and sustain relationships with children, men, family and neighbours. Truly to understand the experience of mothers and mothering is to look beyond the mother–child relationship to the social forces and policies that shape and restrain its expression. Looked at in this way, the experience of becoming a mother and caring for children is not inevitable, biologically dictated or a private matter unconnected to the rest of society, but is the result of social organisation. The isolation is socially engineered, the result of policies and institutionalised practices, some of which are located in social service agencies. That which is socially organised can be altered; the institution of motherhood is not fixed for all time in its present form.

'Fit mothering' and assessment

Child care, particularly child protection, is seen as highly skilled and priority work. Open access provision for children and parents has been undermined by economic constraints on state-funded services. This means that, in families and local communities where there is high unemployment, there is little to supplement family resources. Where this exists, it is more likely to come through action on health, education and anti-poverty or community regeneration programmes than from social services departments. The policy levers and the resources to promote public health and social well-being, including good parenting, are through corporate strategies in the local authority, the criminal justice system and regional initiatives.

These initiatives sit alongside policies emphasising parental responsibility for children's behaviour and the control of adolescents, and are likely to be of primary concern for social and care workers. In poorly resourced environments, additional burdens fall on women. The conditions in which children are being brought up all too often involve an inadequate income with little or no access to the resources that can relieve mothers of virtually total responsibility. Even when a man is part of the family, women are seen, and see themselves, as being the person primarily responsible for child care.

Caring for disabled children falls mainly on their mothers. They are less likely to be in employment than are the mothers of families without a disabled child, and they have to cope with contacts with health professionals and with the additional costs (Cavet, 1998; Lawton, 1998). Where black children are involved, the difficulties are compounded because the young person's blackness can be ignored as the concentration is on the disability (Begum and Gillespie-Sells, 1993).

The statutory responsibilities of social service agencies are to a large extent centred on the care, protection and control of children and young people. A complex of laws and guidance requires workers to enforce minimum standards. The assumption behind these laws, reinforced by the Conservative government's policies and the ideology of the New Right, was that parenting is entirely a private, personal responsibility. Under New Labour in the late 1990s, they are seen as part of a radical restructuring of the welfare state that is increasingly explicit about parenting responsibilities. As we have seen in the late 1990s, as in the late 1980s, parenting is still primarily a woman's responsibility and one which women themselves accept as theirs. Apart from specific aspects of health care and education, and in certain circumstances day care, the acquisition of the social and economic conditions for 'good enough' parenting are assumed to be within the grasp and control of the parents themselves. However, the way in which 'good enough' parenting is conceptualised minimises recognition of the impact of the interaction between the dimensions of race, gender, disability and social class on the social development of the child.

The spotlight falls on mothers as the responsible people, and social work and social care concur with the judgement. Mothers are often held responsible for protecting their children from further abuse (DoH, 1995a). This finding is a practical illustration of how the concept of the 'fit mother' operates. In most instances, the idea of the 'fit mother' is more implicit than explicit. What is a fit mother? Each of us needs to be clear about the components, even though the idea is a developing and changing one. The cultural ideal contains the following components and abilities:

- To provide adequate housing, warmth and food
- To provide access to appropriate stimulation and learning opportunities

- To provide suitable discipline, control and moral guidance
- To reproduce feminine and masculine identities in girls and boys
- To possess the characteristic of responsiveness to children
- To have the ability to suppress or delay gratification of one's own needs over long periods
- To provide uninterrupted caring and loving
- To be heterosexual
- To establish and maintain over a long period a monogamous relationship with a man, preferably the biological father, who will provide economic support for the family
- To secure an adequate income for the family, either solely through her own labour or through a man.

For black women, the concept of the 'fit mother' has additional elements. First, it is Eurocentric in minimising the importance of the extended kin and neighbourhood to the family. Second, stereotypes can apply to the way in which black women are seen to provide care ceaselessly for their children. Afro-Caribbean women can be seen as either too harsh in their discipline or alternatively too lax, while Asian women can been seen as overprotective and providing so much caring that it becomes repressive.

The social construction of disability, as we have seen, means that the focus is on disabled women as being the cause of additional responsibilities for children rather than on a lack of adequate personal support for the mother herself. This framework can mean that women with disabilities can be seen, by implication, as less than 'fit mothers' (Keith and Morris, 1996).

Motherhood, in our view, is becoming more tightly structured, and the concept of 'fit mother' is becoming more tightly defined. Social and care workers, along with medical personnel, health visitors, teachers, social security officers and housing workers, monitor mothering from antenatal care onwards into parenting education. In the main, this is likely to mean mothering education. The concept of the 'fit mother' is used by courts when assessing the offences committed by women. It is not the offence alone that is judged but the appropriateness of the behaviour for a person who is, or may become, a rearer of the next generation (Carlen and Worrall, 1987).

There is no corresponding 'fit father' role for workers to use in their assessment and planning. A number of changes are taking place that impinge indirectly on the role of the father. There are increasing arguments from men for new rights as fathers when an increasing number of children are being born outside marriage, and for rights for fathers who are separated from children because of divorce. Similarly, the state, through the Child Support Agency, has begun to set some markers around the financial responsibilities that men carry when they leave children in one family to live either in another or alone. In spite of these changes, little substance is added to the concept of the 'fit father' that would support its use in practice. The Child Support Agency seems to have further disadvantaged women who have left abusive or unsupported relationships as they can be penalised for not revealing the name of the father. In effect, an additional responsibility is being added to the category of 'fit mother', that is, a responsibility to declare the father.

Whether or not men contribute toward their families financially, emotionally or personally through making time available to be with the children, they rarely lose their rights of access to, and authority over, children. Unlike motherhood, workers are not expected, and do not expect, to monitor or improve expressions of fatherhood in the families they visit. This remains the case even though, in families where the man is unemployed, he may be encouraged to participate more in order to give him a role when his breadwinning function is lost. The consequence is to see the mother as the person on whom to concentrate. She is held responsible for breakdowns or failures in any area of a child's life and at any age, whether it occurs in the home, the neighbourhood or the school, in employment or during unemployment. Family Group Conferences are a means of trying to renegotiate this imbalance of responsibility, but they have yet to become part of mainstream practice.

Day care and 'fit mothering'

Parenting, or mothering, is seen now as a difficult and, at times, arduous task. The view of the transmission of poverty through families, of the so-called breakdown of family life and, in particular, of young women as being at risk of pregnancy and young men as being troublesome, and of the drug culture, has led to a reassertion of 'family values' by the UK Labour government in 1997. This includes reducing the benefits available to lone mothers through welfare payments before an infrastructure of day care for children is in place, and exploring various ways to support the two-parent family as the 'ideal'. There is support for the 1960s calls for education for parenthood (National Commission of Inquiry into the

Prevention of Child Abuse, 1996). Courses in schools aim to prepare young people for this role, and there are calls for education on parenting and personal relationships to become part of the national curriculum. Day care is another means of relieving some of the pressures on mothers and teaching parenting skills to women who come into contact with social services agencies at the same time as increasing children's access to resources for play and learning.

Locally based provision for children, mothers and, in areas of high unemployment, fathers is seen as one of the means of relieving women whose life conditions may include social isolation, of some of the burdens of looking after children when living in poverty and poor housing. From 1979 to 1997, publicly funded day care concentrated on a tiny minority of children defined as being at risk because social policy viewed raising children as a parental responsibility. In the late 1990s, this is changing. Key government policies are accessing employment as the way out of poverty, together with education and training to produce and maintain a skilled workforce. 'Child care' has come to mean day care for the children of working parents and is complementary to welfare to work programmes. It is an area in which the state has accepted some limited responsibility with parents and puts the UK in line with other parts of Europe.

Prior to 1997, a few community nurseries went against a policy that defined day care as a private activity of mothers to be financed by them, often through employment. A number of the women using day care are the staff of social service agencies, although only a minority use private nurseries as a means of providing day care for their children (Balloch *et al.*, 1995, 1998). Black women and the mothers of disabled children have the additional requirements of ensuring that carers do not discriminate against the children or undermine their sense of identity. For the majority of women, day care continues to be provided through family, relatives, friends, neighbourhood play schemes and local groups. In addition, there is a large but unknown number of unregistered daily minders.

The ideology of 'fit mothering' requires that women provide all care for the very young child apart from on exceptional occasions. Extensive, well-conducted research demonstrating the capacity of young children to relate to more than one carer has not shifted this belief (Rutter, 1981), including among women themselves. The evidence shows the main conditions for success as being that the person likes children and cares about the particular child. Given the ideology of a mother's responsibility, it is not surprising that there continues to be a marked lack of day care for the under 3s, or that employment, but not unemployment, is seen as a problem for mothers. The reverse situation applies to fathers: unemployment, but not employment, is seen as a problem. Yet some women are thought to be good mothers even though, or because, they do not care continuously for their children. A system of au pairs, nannies and boarding school enables women with the economic means totally, or partially, to separate caring about their children from the tasks of caring for or tending them (Parker, 1981). Because of their class position, the mothers who use this class-related system to care for their children are not viewed as inadequate by the state. Pressures on lone mothers to move off benefits into employment, however, is part of an attempt to extend a favourable view of working women to include the poorest mothers and children in society. The issue is whether women are forced back into unacceptable marriages and relationships in the name of 'family values' either because they do not have the skills to earn sufficient to support themselves and their children alone or because there are not the jobs available.

Women who use state services or voluntary provision, either because they recognise that they cannot give day-to-day care or because they are assessed to have fallen below the minimum standard of care, are viewed extremely negatively, as are women on benefits (Beresford and Turner, 1997). They also frequently view themselves in the same way. The result when child care is shared with the state is that problems are created for both the child and the parent. Sharing care, even for parts of the day, raises the question of the children's needs and how these can be balanced against those of the mother. This formulation of the problem places the requirement on the woman to take, or demand, just enough space for herself, but not so much that it is deemed to be detrimental to the child. Similarly, workers who consider it important for women to have space for themselves in order to be aware of and meet their own needs are faced with the question of balance. The definition of the needs of women and their children as conflicting is made within the institution of motherhood:

> Women have been made the main parties in that conflict, so that it can look as if women's freedom is necessarily threatening to children, while children's care necessarily requires women to set their personal sights low. (New and David, 1985, p. 328)

This persists even though women are now expected to combine care and employment.

One practical effect of this conflict in the lives of women is that, in career terms, it is an advantage for a man, but a disadvantage for a woman, to be married. The question of balance in meeting children's needs, and, as we shall see later, those of men, does not arise for a single or a married man. A woman has to remain both single and childless to ensure that it does not arise for her.

Involuntary childlessness

The negative social value placed on childlessness is a part of the experience of being a woman and of becoming a mother: 'Involuntary childlessness in women is seen as a tragedy and voluntary childlessness at least an oddity' (New and David, 1985, p. 41). More single women are having, and keeping, their babies than in the past. The decline in the number of babies for adoption over the past 20 years, along with an intense pronatalist ideology, means that workers in social service agencies are now meeting few women who are childless. They meet ever fewer women who are voluntarily childless, in part because the number is relatively small and in part because social services in all sectors are set up as a family-based service.

Unlike their colleagues in other agencies, social workers in hospital settings, including genetic counsellors, routinely see women applying for, or referred for, high-technology pre- and post-conception interventions. The diagnostic redefinition of infertility from 2 to 1 year or less of unprotected heterosexual activity, along with the development of new reproductive technologies, means that more women are seen in infertility clinics (Hanmer, 1997). The human genome project has increased the number of women undergoing amniocentesis and other tests for genetic conditions. The precise number of infertile women depends upon the definition of the condition and the exclusion of the number who are intentionally childless. The initial claim that up to 20 per cent of women are infertile combines those who do not intend to have children with those who do. Among the younger generation of women, there is a proportion who do not, at this stage in their lives, see children as essential to their fulfillment as a woman and state that they do not intend to have children at all (Wilkinson and Mulgan, 1995). Whether this conscious decision to remain childless will persist into later adulthood has yet to be seen, but this position is in marked contrast to that of women who undergo extensive and often distressing treatment to conceive, more often than not without success (Klein, 1989).

Our social policy is structured on an assumption that people should live in biologically based nuclear families. This assumption is so pervasive that it is largely unquestioned, and unquestionable. The brief of the Seebohm Report (1968) was to advise on the organisation of social services as a family-based service. This objective is implicit in the Barclay Report (1982), where community care is described as family care. Although there is a reduction in the popularity of marriage, most couples who begin by living together eventually marry or end their relationship (Utting, 1995). These trends are particularly marked among younger women. Observation suggests that, both prescriptively and statistically, the small family is the norm. In the public image, marriage, parenthood and the family are inextricably linked and prescribed avenues for those wishing join 'the mature, the secure, the respectable and the adult' (Campbell, 1985).

Women who are without children, either from choice or because they cannot have a child biologically, are rarely the concern of social services agencies, although this situation applies to a number of workers in them. In particular, women in senior managerial positions in social service departments are likely to be childless, divorced or single (Balloch *et al.*, 1995). Living with or without children is one of the commonalities and also diversities between women who use services and those providing them.

The main concern of workers for women living without children ironically remains with mothers, that is, the women who are separated from their children, either because these mothers are offenders and in prison, are ill or addicted to drugs or alcohol, or have not met the standards of 'fit mothering'. Justifications for removing children from women can involve economic or social factors as well as negative assessments of mother–child interactions. For example, the risk of being physically removed from giving care to their children is high for women who are persistent offenders. They are also high for lesbian mothers regardless of the standard of care being provided. At the end of the women's lives, they can become the concern of social service agencies because their children have died before them or live at a distance from them.

Another example of the dominance of social factors is provided by children who are removed from mothers whose care is adequate if they are thought unable to control an abusing father or cohabitee. The unconscious assumption that women are responsible for all relationships within the household can mean punitive reactions against mothers once child sexual abuse is discovered, even when the mother reports the offence herself. Her initial disbelief that her husband could be abusing her daughter may be held against her, as may her fear of violence from him as she is unable to guarantee that she can single-handedly evict the man should he come around again (Hanmer and Saunders, 1993).

The recent increase in attention given to the sexual abuse of children, in which almost all offenders are men, raises in an acute form the need to examine ideological assumptions about 'fit mothering' and the lack of a corresponding 'fit fathering' concept. As long as mothers wish to care for their children, the threat and the actual removal of them is a powerful mode of social control and punishment. The assumption that caring is not men's work, and abuse within the family is not 'real' crime, means that men are neither controlled nor punished. These problems will be explored further in the next chapter, but we will first look at the remaining caring functions prescribed for women.

Caring for adults

Care for older people is a significant problem for women. A major concern of governments throughout Europe is how to cope with the economic consequences of increased life expectancy. Between 1971 and 1996, the number of people aged 75 and over rose by more than 60 per cent (SSI, 1995). Between 1992 and 2032 in England and Wales, the number of people aged over 85 is forecast to increase by 126 per cent (OPCS, 1994). Women are the largest proportion of these groups, and widows on pension, together with lone mothers, make up 3 out of 10 of the households on low incomes. How older people are viewed and the path of the long-term care debate are crucial for women, who are the majority of both carers and older people.

The average package of home care remains 5 hours a week whether provided by the statutory or voluntary sector, and charging for this service is the norm. Home care contact hours have grown rapidly, some 31 per cent between 1992 and 1994, and this is enabling more older people to stay at home or with their families for longer periods of time (Local Government Associations, 1995). Eligibility criteria are becoming tighter, and the packages of care that older people receive remain limited and standard rather than flexible and responsive to their particular needs. The vast majority of older people who need care and personal assistance still receive this from family members or their spouse and have no contact with social service agencies.

Most elderly people, including the very elderly and incorporating 45 per cent of those with dementia, live in families, but the political concentration is on a minority of people who need residential or nursing home care at the end of their lives (Holmes *et al.*, 1995). The panic about numbers is subsiding as it is estimated that this number will not increase in the next decade (Harding *et al.*, 1996). Care provided by the family is a highly significant means through which costs to the state are controlled (Schneider *et al.*, 1993). Family carers, as we have seen, are less likely to receive support. In spite of the right of carers to have their needs separately assessed, this does not provide entitlement to even minimum services, although the older person may be as frail and vulnerable as those in residential care (Levin and Moriarty, 1994). Women, as the majority of carers, are particularly vulnerable in a system that is budget driven and where the number of places in day care, residential homes and community services is very limited.

Black women are even more vulnerable to inadequate care when elderly. Ahmad-Aziz and her colleagues (1992, p. 14) describe the position of black women elders:

> Such a woman might experience a triple standard of discrimination, of sexism all her life, compounded by racism and ageism in her later years. Those black women who become frail may be seen of little use either sexually or in terms of their assumed caring functions.

Elderly black women, more than their white counterparts, may experience poverty because of many years in low-paid jobs, extensive family responsibilities and the implications that this has for their pensions. The growing proportion of older people in the black and minority ethnic communities intensifies the need to develop appropriate and culturally sensitive support. Responding to this situation will become increasingly more important for social service agencies.

Debates about long-term care costs must be placed in the broader context of how it is believed that older people should relate to the wider society. The issue turns on what people think those who are older contribute to society. All too often, older people are defined as burdens. This is not a new value judgement or experience in Western society. Older people are often accorded less status in societies that define independence and productivity in terms of employment. Unless other forms of socially valued contribution are recognised, this situation will continue.

Many women have a cycle of caring beginning with caring for children and moving on to caring for elderly relatives and finally aged spouses.

Serial monogamy is a factor affecting the cycle of caring. As women tend to marry men older than themselves, there are, at the end of their lives, a number of women looking after the very old, a substantial proportion of whom will be their husbands. Other women will be looking after relatives, friends or neighbours at the end of their lives. As with caring for children, it is important to recognise that the heaviest burden is likely to fall on working-class women, given that the middle and upper classes are more likely to be able to buy access to resources that relieve the stress of caring.

In addition to performing the bulk of informal care, women are more likely than men to:

- Provide the most intimate of personal care
- Go on caring longer for adults with higher levels of dependency
- Give up work to look after a dependent or dying child or adult.

A recognition of the cycle of caring and its requirements is crucial for assessment and practice. Stages in the cycle may overlap, and women may be simultaneously caring for elderly relatives and children. The potential conflicts that women face in demands for attention and around the allocation of space in houses designated for nuclear family living are familiar to most workers both from their own personal lives and from the lives of the people using services.

Caring for adults is taken to be as natural for women as caring for children. Because this view is often internalised, women blame themselves if the act of caring is unsuccessful. The failure is personalised. In our view, caring for adults, like the institution of motherhood, is socially constructed and needs analysis before it is possible for practice and services to intervene in ways supportive to women. The classic text, appropriately called *A Labour of Love* (Finch and Groves, 1983), identifies through its various chapters the components of caring:

- Caring is composed of two elements:
  - caring about a person (love and feeling for a person)
  - caring for them (washing, feeding, laundering and so on).
  The first form of caring is concerned with emotional aspects, the second with looking after or 'tending'.
- Caring is often hard and laborious.
- Caring must go on irrespective of whether there is love in the first place or whether it continues. As individuals, we may prefer to be

cared for by someone who cares about us, but in residential and day care work, tending someone may precede caring about the person, or it may never happen. The same process, although we do not like to admit it, occurs in families. In certain situations, such as acute sickness necessitating hospital admission, we readily accept the separation of caring about and caring for.

- Caring is about keeping people alive.
- Costs are involved in caring for people. These can be measured in personal terms as relationships with men, children and friends are affected. Living space often becomes cramped, and social life is likely to be restricted. There are also economic costs. While employment is now the norm for women, those caring for dependent adults or handicapped children are less likely to be in work. Not only does caring involve additional costs for items such as heating, laundry and food, but there is also less likelihood of maintaining living standards through having two wages. The assumption behind social policy that the man is the breadwinner while the woman is available at home clearly does not now fit the facts of women's lives, though it underpins community care and budgets. Without the sacrifices of women, community care could not possibly work.
- There is a bias against women in the way in which community resources are allocated both to the carer and to the person needing support. Men are not expected, and do not expect, to do as much as women when caring for another or in looking after themselves. Women are expected, and expect, to do more for themselves and others than men.
- Women predominate as informal carers. 'Correct ideas' about femininity and masculinity support sex role divisions in which caring for adults is seen and experienced as a woman's duty. In spite of mass unemployment affecting the lives of many men and the fact that paid work is now a part of the majority of women's lives, women are believed to be, and often believe themselves to be, the appropriate people to take on this unpaid labour.

Care and social policy

Even if care is given within an emotional relationship, it remains work. Social policies ignore the element of labour: for example, current practice is to withdraw services from an older person when he or she moves into the home of a relative; the assessment is likely to be that the person is no longer at risk. If we are to take seriously the needs of the carer and the work of caring, along with the vulnerability of the elderly person that necessitated the move, services should at least be maintained if not increased at this point.

While policies have changed to encourage women's employment, the care of adults remains, for the vast majority of women, a private concern to be carried out in those places where intimate relations with women are found (Graham, 1984, p. 16). The state intervenes only in emergencies, when families or friends are no longer able to cope on their own or when there is no family. To turn to the state for support is to admit failure on the part of the caring woman as no collective responsibility is accepted beyond being a last-resort safety net.

The economic pressures of an older population, and the greater instability of marriage both in terms of durability and as an economic unit, mean that social services may in future increasingly have a role in supporting women in combining caring and paid employment. This contrasts with the past, when the primary focus was to monitor women in their caring roles. Economic and demographic trends have pushed this social policy towards:

1. Removing the impediments to employment for women as mothers – through day care – and women as carers through family-friendly policies in the workplace and strategies to provide reliable support. This investment is worthwhile because carers of adults 'save' the state about £31 billion per year
2. Economic restructuring, which requires two incomes rather than one if family poverty is to be tackled
3. The impact of caring on pension rights and re-entry into the workplace, resulting in poverty in retirement
4. A recognition of civic rights for disabled people to live independently and for them to employ their own personal assistants.

All these developments influence the form taken by these relationships of love and work arising out of the structuring of women's relations with men. This is the theme of the next chapter.

Questions

1. Do you agree that all the qualities listed earlier in the chapter are necessary or desirable to be a 'fit mother'? If you disagree or wish to

qualify any of the qualities on this list, why and how?

2. What implications does your list have for black and minority ethnic women, disabled women and women with learning difficulties?

3. Think of the children you have witnessed being taken into public care. Were there economic or social factors, including race and gender, as well as negative mother–child interactions in these decisions?

4. How have women in your family been affected by the cycle of care?

5. Think of your experience involving the support needs of adults within the family. What help is given to the person who assumes primary responsibility?

6. Have you observed differential resource allocation when carers are men rather than when women are black rather than white? If yes, do you think that any factors other than gender or race were involved in these decisions?

7. What qualities do you think are important for 'fit fathering'?

8. Before proceeding to the next chapter, have you any views on why women's relationships with men are so important in determining the nature of women's work?

5

Living with Men

The interpersonal problem most frequently presented by women using services concerns their relations with men. These are primarily focused on relationships with the family, but, as we shall see in Chapter 7, relationships between male and female colleagues are also problematic for women workers. This chapter draws attention to the relationship between wife and child abuse, the prevalence and incidence of violence against women and children, the resources around which marriage relations are structured, divorce as a means of reformulating marriage, and problems and issues in achieving women-centred practice.

Why women's relationships with men are an issue for social work and social care

Although not one of the statutory responsibilities, relationships with men must be a significant focus of any practice that aims to be women centred. Men figure prominently in the lives of many women using services and may even be identified as a major problem for these women, but how are we to understand the lack of response to requests for help from women with problems with men? Almost all women marry or spend many years of their lives in heterosexual relationships. Almost all women have in common the experience of being a wife at some time in their lives and of being house workers. We share these experiences with our women service users. Living with and caring for men is held to be the central focus of a woman's life and is a prerequisite for caring for children. Many women strive to marry, to have children and, depending upon their ethnic background, to live in either a nuclear family setting or an extended household.

As the experiences we have of caring for men range from the positive to the negative, we need to look more closely at our expectations and the position of women in marriage, because social policy and practice are closely bound up with preserving and creating particular forms of interpersonal behaviour and relationship. A negative impact on women's physical and mental health is created by:

- The isolation of many women's labour in the home and the lack of a close personal relationship with their husband/partner
- Husbands who do not, or who only marginally, contribute to the work of maintaining the home
- Violence against women by husbands or partners.

Marriage is better for men's mental health than women's.

Violence against women and children

Violence against mothers by husbands or partners and other male family relations may occur along with child abuse. Violence against mothers should be looked for in investigations of child physical, sexual and emotional abuse (Cleaver and Freeman, 1995). There is growing attention to the impact of violence against their mothers on the health, sexual and emotional well-being, educational attainment and development of children who witness violence (World Bank, 1993).

The connections between abuse to mothers and to children are often missed in practice because the concentration is solely on the child. Understanding about violence and its impact on family members is important for both women-centred and child-centred practice (Mullender, 1996). To assist mothers who are experiencing violence is to help children who are abused (Mullender and Morley, 1994; Saunders, 1995). It is not necessary for children to be directly assaulted to be harmed by violence. The harm to children of witnessing and knowing about violence to their mothers is part of child protection. Children need the opportunity to talk about how witnessing and knowing about violence to their mothers has harmed them. It is not sufficient simply to assist children and their mothers to move from violent homes, although this is more often than not the first step to a better life.

Violence against women is being raised in a European and world context. Discussions at this level focus on universal issues of women's rights as human rights and cross-national forms of abuse. This focus emerges from United Nations resolutions and activities, such as the Women's Conference in Beijing in 1995. A multinational examination of violence against women raises issues of pornography and trafficking in women as human rights' violations (Elman, 1996). Both private and public forms of violence, such as sexual harassment in the workplace and family-based violence, are linked to social phenomena. Violence against women is a citizenship issue, with a small, but growing international literature on good practice as well as research and political activities (United Nations Office, 1993; Hanmer, 1996). Welfare workers around the world are responding to men's violence against women and children.

A central plank of New Right theory in the 1980s was that the growing independence of women from men was undermining both children and men by displacing men from their rightful place within the family. Women and marriage gave men a place and responsibilities that calmed, or in traditional parlance tied, them down through family life. Far from diminishing, this view is becoming more widespread with a backlash against feminism and arguments about new inequalities that are emerging for men:

> the fear [is] that the gender issue has now come full circle with men the new victims, discriminated against by a legislative framework of equal opportunities, and a climate of political correctness which skews power too much in the direction of women and an economic climate which needs their skills. (Wilkinson, 1994, p. 47)

Sexual abuse and harassment by men is counterpoised with that by women, even though the incidence is tiny in comparison. While abuse and harassment by men or women is unacceptable, in the vast majority of cases the abuse of power is by men. The argument, not the fact, is a renewed effort by men to hold on to the power they appear to be losing in their relationships with women. Marriage is at its lowest level since records began, but there is no serious indication that heterosexuality as a social or a sexual practice is endangered (Utting, 1995).

Prevalence and incidence of violence against women and children

Workers are likely to encounter, both knowingly and unknowingly, a high incidence of violence against women in their homes as it is widely spread throughout all social classes and ethnic groups (Mayhew *et al.*, 1993; Hanmer, 1995). During the 1990s, major incidence and prevalence studies were undertaken both nationally and locally. For example, in

1992 there were a minimum of 530,000 domestic physical assaults involving male partners, ex-partners, household members and other relatives in England and Wales. The location of attacks was almost always in or just outside the woman's home. Violence against women in their homes by the men with whom they live, or are closely associated, is likely to be the most common form of violent crime.

Workers have to be aware that surveys use different bases to calculate violence against women. The British Crime Surveys define violence as physical assaults only. A study of physical and sexual violence in marriage found that 28 per cent of a representative sample of over 1000 married women in the UK said that they had been hit within their marriages, just over one-half of divorced and separated women had been hit by their husbands, and 1 in 8 women reported non-consensual sexual relations or rape (Painter, 1991). Several local studies produced more detailed information drawing attention to the range of situations that women find threatening, harassing and violent both in and outside their homes (Hanmer and Saunders, 1993). These range from indecent exposure, insulting or threatening behaviour, obscene or threatening telephone calls, physical and sexual assault, battery, breach of the peace, abduction and criminal damage to property including arson. An Islington survey (Mooney, 1993) asked about both violence and abuse over the previous year and over the women's total life span. Looking at lifetime experiences, mental cruelty, which includes verbal abuse, being deprived of money, clothes or sleep, and being prevented from going out, was experienced by 37 per cent of women, threats of violence by 27 per cent, actual physical violence by 32 per cent, injuries by 27 per cent and rape or non-consensual sex by 23 per cent.

Age is systematically related to attacks, younger women being more likely to experience violence in their homes. Pregnancy or having dependent children is associated with violence from men with whom women have or have had a close relationship. As women are never more dependent on men than when they are pregnant and their children are young, the conclusion drawn by Hanmer and Saunders is that women's dependency on men is the key factor in assaults by men on women. This makes it easier for men to abuse women without fear of retaliation, such as their leaving. This dependency can be financial and emotional, and it is socially valorised through widely held views on family life. Socially, it is much less acceptable to leave men, whatever their behaviour, after children are born.

The other way of calculating the extent of violence against women is through reporting rates to the police. Between 2 and 20 per cent of domestic-based incidents are reported to the police. These variations reflect the accuracy of police recording practices and age-related residential patterns. Information from police attendances and victimisation surveys conservatively suggest that approximately 10 per cent of women in any large population are assaulted in any one year, that is, 10,000 if a city has 100,000 women over the age of 16 years.

Workers encountering an incident of domestic violence have to be aware of the repeated nature of domestic violence. Half the women who reported domestic assaults for the first time experienced more than one offence within the year (Hanmer and Griffiths, 1998).

Estimates of the number of men who directly abuse both their wives and their children vary between one-third and over one-half (Canadian Panel on Violence Against Women, 1993; Mullender and Morley, 1994; Cleaver and Freeman, 1995). Furthermore, almost all children living in households where their mothers are being physically and/or sexually assaulted know this, and many have the experience of being physically present when their mothers are being attacked. Children respond differently to violence against their mothers depending on their age, sex, stage of development, role in the family, disability and ethnicity. Children, even very young children, frequently try to help their mothers by trying to stop their father's attacks, by running for help or by aiding their mothers after an attack. Some children may be too frightened to do so and cower in their rooms or, if in bed, hide their heads under the bedclothes, or they may stand watching while screaming and expressing distress in other ways. Gendering family members is important as the family displays differential power relations between mother and father and also relates differently to male and female children. This is why we must be careful about making bland references to 'parents' and 'children' as these ideas mask important differences within families (Frost and Stein, 1989, p. 8). These differences can affect how boys and girls respond to attacks on their mothers and the meaning it has for them.

Since the 1980s, there has been a surge of interest in professional circles in the sexual abuse of young children. In the vast majority of cases, the survivor is a girl and the abuser a male known to her, often from her own family (Nelson, 1987; Kelly, 1998). Rape Crisis and Women's Aid have called attention to sexual abuse as a feature present in women's lives for many years (Hague *et al.*, 1996). The estimate that between 1 in 2 and 1 in 10 women was sexually abused as a child came as no surprise to the agencies, nor did the fact that learning to survive violence and its threat is part of most women's life skills. These issues are high on the agenda of women workers, who are sensitive to the gender perspectives of their clients' lives and their own.

While statistical studies are particularly well developed in economically developed nations, women's groups are active globally irrespective of culture, religion, political regimes and other variations between national states. For example, the Canadian Violence Against Women survey found the same patterns as in the UK studies (Canadian Panel on Violence Against Women, 1993). Leaving violent men does not necessarily end the attacks on women and children. Abuse after marriages have ended is more likely to make women fear for their lives (Canadian Panel on Violence Against Women, 1993; Wilcox, 1996).

One of the strategies women use to escape continuous abuse after separation is to move home. The search for safer accommodation disrupts the social support networks of women and the educational continuity of children. However willing social service agencies are to support women, there are well-known difficulties when moving involves crossing the geographical boundaries of organisations. We know of no research on this, but Parker (1995) found that families with disabled children who were geographically mobile were less well served than those who did not move home. We have no reason to think that women and their children who move to escape violence are any better served. Agencies within the same locality are often unaware of each other's interventions and even less likely to know of the previous involvement of agencies in other geographical areas (Hanmer, 1995).

As the impact of social and emotional violence becomes more clearly identified, it is increasingly a concern for all agencies with responsibility for promoting health and social well-being within communities. The Zero Tolerance campaign against violence began in Edinburgh and has been adopted by a growing number of local authorities in the UK as well as abroad. Zero Tolerance poster campaigns, following the public education strategies developed around alcohol, drugs and other harmful activities, draw attention to the extent, types and unacceptability of violence against women and children. The aim is to explain how personal behaviour needs to change, not only for the benefit of individuals, but also for the community.

Resources for structuring marriage relations

Women-centred practice means looking at the science of power within relationships between men and women. Marriage relations can be seen as having four resources through which husbands and wives structure their relationships with each other: economic resources, force and its threat, status, and love and friendship (Goode, 1971). Although an old reference, this remains relevant in describing the types of resource available in the family, and Chapter 6 describes how the distribution of these resources is changing. Men may have more of all four of these resources when their wider social contacts, that is their families of origin, friends and acquaintances, and formal agencies, are considered (Hanmer, 1995; Hearn, 1994; Wilcox, 1996). Women and their children are often more socially isolated and draw their major support from each other.

Economic resources

Domestic labour is another form of social reproduction. By cleaning, by feeding and, some argue, even by intimate personal behaviour, including sexual servicing, women reproduce the labour force by enabling men to return daily to their place of work. Christine Delphy (1984) argues that this invisible financial contribution of the unwaged work of women exposes the inaccuracy of the belief that women are maintained by their husbands. The so-called domestic labour debate examined how women bring the equivalent of income into the family through the domestic production of goods and services. When women are in paid employment, their wages are almost always used on family rather than personal expenditure (World Bank, 1993), providing for their own and their families' upkeep as well as making an invisible financial contribution through unwaged domestic work.

The wife, in caring for her husband so that he may return to the paid workforce refreshed and able to carry on another day, is contributing to the Gross National Product, although this is not counted in reckoning the amount of goods and services produced in society. This issue was raised by many women from round the world at the United Nations Decade on Women Conferences in Nairobi, Kenya, in July 1985 and at the World Conference on Women in Beijing in 1995. A resolution calling on government to count the labour of housewives in the Gross National Product was passed at the official conference. While this development may have important psychological benefits, the husband will continue to be able to exercise control over his wife and her labour through the allocation of household finance (Homer *et al.*, 1984; Pahl, 1989). If we look at those who are unemployed and in receipt of pensions, unemployment or other benefit, the man is deemed by the state to be head of the household and receives payment for himself and his wife. The norm is that women are dependent on men.

The four systems for allocating money in the home are the whole-wage system, the allowance system, the pooling system and the independent management system (Pahl, 1989). In the whole-wage system, the man hands over all of his wage packet, and the wife manages their financial affairs, which includes giving him a small amount for his personal needs. In the allowance system, the husband gives his wife a housekeeping allowance for specific items, such as food and possibly items such as the children's clothing, gas or electricity, and so on. The pooling system usually involves a joint bank account and is a 'share and share alike' method. In the independent management system, husbands and wives manage their money separately and each makes payments for particular items of household expenditure.

These four basic systems are enlarged by the work of Homer *et al.* (1984), who have examined the money allocation systems of women coming into the Women's Aid refuge in Cleveland. There are two additional systems. In the first the woman receives no money whatsoever from her husband: the whole wage is his. In the second, the woman is handed the wage packet or allowance but must give back money whenever it is demanded. Money distribution is a greater problem when money is short. There is a relationship between women's working patterns and the control of family income by men. Where men had total control over family income, no women went out to work, 'a factor which apparently both aided and grew out of their husband's dominance' (Homer *et al.*, 1984, p. 11). Alternatively, when women were in paid employment, husbands reduced the money they gave to their wives or expected them to take on additional financial responsibilities.

It is very important for workers to enquire about money allocation as women may be without any or have too low an income to maintain their current living arrangements. Women may be living below benefit levels or have no money whatsoever as even their child benefit may be taken by their husbands. Women may turn to family for help, for example to their mothers for meals for themselves and their children. This solution, however, is rarely permanent, and if men continue to refuse to treat their earnings or benefits as a family wage, women may be driven into refuges. Many women in refuges express great relief and pleasure at having more money, over which they genuinely have control for themselves and their children once on benefits in their own right.

Once on benefits, however, women's economic problems can take other forms: the threat and practice of cutting off welfare benefits, or of being monitored and questioned by officials, and the Benefits Agency's attempts to collect any or more money from the fathers of their children, are persistent worries for many women. Women who are thought to be cohabiting with other men will lose their income and this can restrict an already socially isolated woman in forming new relationships. Whilst working mainly with women who are poor, there has been a reluctance to focus on money as a source of conflict in the household, but charges for social care inevitably involve workers in finance. Understanding how economic resources are allocated within the household becomes a focus for work generally and not only in woman-centred practice.

Many of the women who use services will not be able to bring economic power into their relationship with men. Constant worries about money can contribute to stressful relationships, separation and divorce, and violence (Kempson, 1996). Individual responses vary widely: women may stay in violent relationships in order to protect their children from even greater poverty, or some younger mothers may prefer independent motherhood on the grounds that a permanent relationship with a man who has few job prospects gives them and their children little security (Rogers and Rogers, 1996).

Force and its threat as a resource

The use of threat and force as a last resort resource, that is, to be used only after all else has failed, is not the correct way to understand this factor. Men may use the threat of force, and force itself, independently of the acquisition of other resources and in preference to gentler methods of control. This may be linked with an understanding of masculinity, that is, of what being a 'real' man is about, or it may be simply that, as a husband, he can get away with the use of force provided he only attacks his wife. Wives have been defined as the appropriate victims of violence (Dobash and Dobash, 1980).

Even when violent assault in marriage was thought to be very unusual, workers were always more aware than the general public of the extent and type of violence that women might experience in marriage. The latter half of the nineteenth century was a time of widespread knowledge about the abuse of women and girls in Britain, particularly of women in or accused of prostitution, in domestic service as well as in marriage (Jeffreys, 1985). The physical and sexual abuse endured by women was seen to result from their social and legal status and not to be a problem suffered by a few inadequate or abnormal individuals. Considerable effort went into effecting legislative change that gave women the same rights to state protection as were enjoyed by men.

It seems that the knowledge of violence to women as a social issue dwindled with every legislative victory. From 1882 onwards, women gradually gained control over their own earnings and inheritances. The extensions of women's rights, although initially in a very limited fashion, to separation, divorce, maintenance and the custody of children changed many aspects of marital relations. The age of consent was raised from 12 to 16 years, and finally the law on incest was passed in 1908 (Coveney *et al.*, 1984). The right to vote was achieved by the first wave of feminism, and, in the agitation just before World War I, there was a resurgence, although smaller than that in the latter half of the nineteenth century, of public consciousness about violence to women. Votes for women were seen as a way of accomplishing many aims, including the control of male violence. It was believed that a full enfranchised female population would ensure the legislation needed to enable all women to have a decent life.

Love and friendship as a resource

Love and friendship, the sole resource that women are more likely to have more of than men within the heterosexual family, are gained by a lifelong devotion to men, children and kin. The subordination of women is rooted in their servicing role by living through and for others. Yet at moments of crisis, the affections of others may be there to sustain the wife's point of view. This resource, however, is double-edged. It is all a woman can hope for, yet, once received and given, it confirms a woman's subordinate social position. Through a love of their husbands, homes and children, women are inducted into a relationship characterised by dependency on the male (Hanmer, 1978; Leonard Barker, 1980). In this way love, too, becomes a mechanism for the control of women by men.

Violence against women and their children demonstrates that the basic requirements for a good wife need not be reciprocated for a man to be seen as a good enough husband and father. This means that social support for women may not be forthcoming from others as a man's standing as a good enough son, husband and father may not require that he place his affections, loyalties, income and time with his wife, while she will be expected to do this in relation to him in order to continue to receive the support of others. She cannot necessarily depend upon the unaltering support of others, whether family, friends or workmates. Supportive interventions may be ambiguous, contradictory and erratic. If she is lucky, she will have consistent, substantial support from at least one other source. Whatever the husband's behaviour, he is likely to retain at least some support, which can be expressed as encouragement or non-intervention (Wilcox, 1996; Hanmer, 1997).

Relationships of deference

It is usual to argue that the culture of deference has disappeared in Britain and that, in relation to women, 'girl power' predominates. These assumptions do not necessarily apply in relationships with men, particularly within the family. Deference operates often in very subtle ways, even when we would prefer to think that it does not, particularly in our own relationships. It remains useful for understanding the pattern of relationships between women and men in the 1990s. Media attention is regularly given to alternative family forms in which couples negotiate family roles and resist conventional prescriptions. These, however, are more rare than the media would lead one to believe.

The majority of people, particularly those who are older, subscribe to conventional views about family life and gender roles irrespective of their race and culture. A significant proportion who subscribe to an alternative view still operate along conventional lines in their relationships (Dench, 1996). It is important to observe what happens as well as to listen to what is said about relationships.

All four resources are present even when styles of marriage vary. Men and women may attempt to share all aspects of married life so that there is minimal role division between them, or role differentiation may be total, so that what a man does a woman does not do and vice versa. Both patterns are subject to the same status differentials between men and women, although the implications of this are expressed differently. With shared roles, women are more likely to carry greater responsibility for how the sharing is to be organised, for example who is to pick up the children from school or stay at home with them if they are ill, while with highly differentiated roles, women undertake activities defined as less prestigious because women do them. In both situations, women are likely to undertake more work than the men with whom they live. That these two extremes are not true opposites may not be evident until something goes wrong in a relationship, when, for different reasons and in different ways, women can find themselves at a disadvantage.

The term 'deferential dialectic' is used to characterise relationships between husbands and wives (Bell and Newby, 1976). Status differentials underpin deferent behaviour, as does the actual power to enforce it. The acceptance of the status differentials that are inherent in being male and female makes the deferent behaviour of wives to husbands seem 'normal'. Both men and women may share the same values, although the expression of deferent behaviour may vary between marriages. For example, a woman may be allowed to go out to a previously agreed place, such as to her relations, provided that she, or someone else, provides or leaves her husband's tea in the oven. Women often interpret this type of response from their husbands as positive, as an indication of a 'good' husband. Women who become active in community groups or in employment to the degree that it impinges on expectations about a woman's behaviour may have to devise various strategies to obtain time away from home.

Women in collective action

The refusal by men to contribute to domestic tasks and to cooperate with child care arrangements were two of the most commonly experienced means by which men effectively restricted the access of women to time and space for leisure. By refusing to participate in this work, or by changing arrangements at the last minute, men are able to regulate the movements of women outside the home and the ways in which time is spent inside the home. Playing on women's guilt feelings is a particularly prevalent form of control. Women may feel guilty because they have not ironed or not cleaned up or not read to their child in order to get an hour for themselves. Other strategies range from petty forms of behaviour, sulking or having a face on through to the explicit exercise of male authority in forbidding the woman to go out. This can be backed up by threatened or actual violence. Men can set limits to the freedom of the women with whom they live, either overtly as 'You may not...' or 'Other women can, but not my wife', or more covertly so that a wife indirectly seeks permission through some form of consultative process with her husband. Restricting the access of women to the public space enables men to control the way in which women use time in the home as well as outside it. Even though there is some individual variation, a wife does not have the same legitimated authority to limit her husband's time away from home, be it spent with his mates after work in the pub or in other company or another place. Nor does a wife have the same authority to enforce how her husband uses his time when at home.

The pattern established within the relationship is likely to persist when the woman becomes disabled or frail because of ill-health and needs care. Violence and abusive behaviour towards women can continue or begin with disability and age. The degree of need for externally provided support will vary with how the man sees his responsibilities as a husband or partner. While some men take caring for disabled or ill partners very seriously, the gendered nature of the care task, coupled with psychologically and physically damaging behaviour, is a significant issue as more people survive to a greater age. The inverse care law comes into operation – those with access to informal care are less likely to receive support (Harding *et al*., 1996). This means that at least some women will be neglected within situations assessed as having the potential for adequate personal care.

Divorce: reformulating marriage

Divorce is not so much the absence of marriage as marriage by another name. Divorce regulates the financial claims that wives and husbands can make on each other, and, when there are children, it regulates contact, residence, care and control, and guardianship. The only right that is extinguished on divorce is that of sexual access. Women can remain, or can become, in great danger from ex-husbands or ex-cohabitees. When relationships break down completely, some women experience their greatest problems with men. Only when there are no children and no ongoing financial payments can divorce truly be seen as legally extinguishing a relationship rather than legally constituting it in a new form.

Divorce led to initiatives to reassert the rights of fathers and husbands within families by re-establishing the so-called traditional family and the access of fathers to their children. Legal initiatives include the Child Support Act 1991, the Children Act 1989 and legislation to make divorce harder to obtain. A review of the literature on the effects on children of divorce indicates that there are a number of factors to take into account in evaluating negative outcomes (Rodgers and Pryor, 1998).The authors conclude that divorce should be seen less as an event than as a process in which a variety of factors influence the outcome for children. These include the degree of conflict between parents and how it and change is managed for themselves and the children. The majority of families in the medium and longer term cope well, but for a significant minority there are risks. These include poverty and poor housing, doing less well in school and behavioural problems. While, in the main, contact with the non-resident parent is positive, the research review alerts its readers to the danger of violence and abuse continuing after divorce. These are statistical relationships and do not predict outcomes faced by individual women. The patterns of related factors can be interrupted by the woman herself and through supportive networks.

Divorce can have positive effects for women and children by eliminating violence and sexual abuse from their lives. Maintaining good relations with both parents is not always possible or desirable for children's well-being. Women and children have experienced major problems caused by professionals (Hester and Radford, 1996) because of a misreading of the Children Act 1989 that contact is more important than safety. This is particularly problematic as violent fathers use contact with children to continue abusing their ex-wives, and mothers become pressurised to agree to unsafe arrangements. Marianne Hester and Lorraine Radford recommend that there should be an end to the presumption by professionals and the courts that contact is in the best interests of a child when there is a history of domestic violence. Contact should only be awarded if it can be shown genuinely to benefit the child and can be safely arranged without posing any threat to the mother .

Holding women responsible for the behaviour of men even after divorce or separation is implicit in the way in which relationships between men and women are constructed. The idea of fit mothering means that, by implication, mothers are blamed, sometimes by the survivors themselves, for not protecting their children against abuse (Wattam and Woodward, 1996). 'Fit fathering' is a patchy concept visible only occasionally, as when the Child Support Agency holds men to economic responsibility for their children. The state interprets divorce as a rewriting of the marriage contract and sets economic support as a criterion of 'fit fathering'.

Black and other minority ethnic women

Relationships with men can be a problem for women from ethnic minorities as well as for women from the dominant culture. Because of racism, black women may be even more reluctant than white women to report incidents to the police or take legal action. This can be because of black women's understanding of the differential response of the criminal justice system to black men and a fear of intensifying the pain inflicted on them by white people (Bernard, 1997). They themselves may be treated unsympathetically by the police. Women are fully aware of what is happening in their communities. Because of racism, black women may find it easier to speak frankly in groups where both cultural differences and racism are fully appreciated. It is important that these opportunities are available since black women may only feel comfortable in certain neighbourhoods where the people of their communities congregate and where culturally relevant services, for example, shops with particular foods or local groups, are available (Butt and Box, 1997).

- There are black and Asian Women's Aid refuges in many cities in Britain to which workers can refer black and Asian women. Run by black and Asian women, they accept unmarried women who wish to leave home as well as women with children.
- White workers can face opposition to offering assistance; they can be made to feel that they should not help Asian women as the male control of women may be said to be an integral part of their culture. White workers can be accused of racism because they are said to be attacking culture. However, Asian cultures, like British culture, are not monolithic. Men and women can have differing views about appropriate behaviour, as can people in different social classes and from different parts of a country. Cultural processes are dynamic, and women, too, form and reform culture.
- Anti-Semitism operates in similar ways. A Jewish women living the traditional orthodox lifestyle may have as many restrictions placed upon her as her Muslim sister. More-assimilated Jewish women, like other women, face social stigma and impending poverty. It is important to remember that not all Jews in Britain are white and that Jewish women face greater social pressures to conform to the ideal family type than do many women in the dominant cultural group. The first Violence Help Line for Jewish Women in Britain began in the 1980s in Leeds, and there is now a Jewish Women's Aid refuge in London

offering help and advice to Jewish women, victims and welfare workers.

- Interpretations of religious teaching can vary among Muslims and Jews as among Christians. Claims that the male control of women is validated by religion is, like culture, contested from within. Workers should not be put off meeting the requests of women for help by accusations that they are attacking religious beliefs by doing so.
- Asian women sometimes prefer to come into white Women's Aid refuges. Determined to leave their homes, they accept that they may be completely cut off from their social group. Asian women who do not speak any English, who have never handled the money and who have almost never been outside their homes, have been rehoused with their children by Women's Aid and learned to cope on their own in a culture they may fear deeply for its racism.
- The fear of racist attacks can keep women from seeking help, as can their fear of the British state (Bernard, 1997).

European data on how black women are disadvantaged draws attention to the requirement that women entering the nation states of Europe from abroad must reside with their husband for a given period of time, in Britain 1 year, in order to demonstrate that the marriage is valid (European Women's Lobby, 1993). If a woman leaves her husband before a year, for any reason including violence from him, she is subject to deportation. After years of organising by Women's Aid, Sahara and other groups to assist individual women, the London-based group Southall Black Sisters has begun a campaign to eliminate this Home Office requirement.

Problems in practice

We now begin to see why workers find it difficult, if not impossible, to respond to requests for help from women having problems with the men with whom they live. The control of women in the home is so normalised that what women are complaining of is the very nature of marriage itself. The conflict that workers feel in their desire to assist unhappy, depressed and even desperate women can lead them simply not to see or not to give much importance to aspects that deeply concern their women clients. Women may be silenced knowing that no-one can help or that no-one wants to help, and their problems may be turned back upon them.

Negative stereotypes of women, the so-called manipulative behaviour of wives, may be the survival skills of the oppressed. We think it important that workers understand why this is happening and the history that is blocking the development of women-centred practice.

The lowest point of public consciousness concerning violence to women was reached in the period immediately after World War II. When conscious knowledge was at its most restricted, the social aspect of the problem was lost, and violence was redefined as the problem of a few individual deviant people and possibly the problem of certain social groups. As the problem became located in the personalities of women, few professional workers saw the abuse of women as requiring action to protect the victim: they thought that women should learn to stop precipitating the violence. These attitudes remain with us today. Maynard's classic study of case records in the North of England in the mid-1980s shows that social workers did not think that physical and sexual attacks on wives were major problems in their marriages (Maynard, 1985). While violence to wives was mentioned in one-third of case files, other factors were seen as 'the problem'. Only in 12 per cent of cases was violence seen as a causative factor in the problems of families and the reason the worker was visiting the woman. Wives were given advice such as 'Don't argue with him too much' and reminded that 'accepting the consequences' was necessary in marriage. If women are seen as deviant in the way in which they look after themselves, for example being described as slovenly, or the husband complains that his wife withholds sex, or he describes the home as a tip, or if he does not like the way the children are cared for, workers feel that they can understand, even if not condone, his subsequent violent actions. This understanding comes from an acceptance of the system of gender stratification. It is unquestioningly accepted that it is the wife's obligation or duty to serve her husband in the manner he views as desirable or necessary.

Violence calls upon workers to have skills in interprofessional work. Many women first respond to repeated matrimonial abuse by going to their doctor, who prescribes tranquillisers or antidepressants (England Research Group, 1984). Now that care in the community is restricting the entry of women into mental hospitals, the role of primary health care becomes even more relevant. The British Crime Survey in 1992 reported that 25 per cent of assaulted women saw their general practitioner (Mayhew *et al.*, 1993). Some women, however, continue to be admitted to mental hospital, and a few either attempt or achieve suicide.

The social and care workers, psychiatrists and others who treat women in hospital or in the community are often unaware that their patients are having difficulty with the men with whom they live. It is not uncommon for women to remain silent about the abuse that has led to professional involvement. They may have tried to tell in the past to no effect, or they may feel that it is of no interest or is beyond the power of the professionals to alleviate. In the past, before the closure of many hospitals, women could use mental hospitals as a place to take a break when unable to cope any longer in an abusive home environment. They, and the staff of the institution, learned to rub along with each other, neither party making strenuous demands on the other. These feelings and behaviour on the part of the women were created and maintained by professional behaviour (Borkowski *et al.*, 1983). The processes by which violence against women is turned back upon the women by the medical profession so that they, rather than the abuse they have received, becomes the problem are explored by Stark *et al.* (1996).

Even if workers do not accept this way of working as correct, given the way in which services are structured and rationed, it is not easy to think through ways that will alter the situation positively for women. Workers can feel frustrated and defeated by the problems that women bring involving relationships with men. This is not just a question of ideology. Women workers are controlled as women by the male members of the service user's family – sometimes by implicit threats. Men workers, too, are met by an unspoken belief on the part of the male head of household that a 'man's home is his castle'. To challenge his 'right' to do as he pleases in his own home may invite violence.

While the social services are approached by women for help in a crisis and become involved longer-term in relation to children, they are unlikely to be the first agency contacted by women (Hanmer, 1995). Social services can be of immediate help, especially through referrals to refuges and homeless accommodation, but in this study of Asian and white women, contact with the social services came through referrals from other agencies, for example the police, educational welfare or health visitors. Social services were invariably involved through child protection, either via the woman's children or her younger siblings, or with her as a child. There was a lesser involvement by social services in the families of Asian women than in white families.

This study also demonstrates damage to relationships with children as a result of violence to women and the ongoing vulnerability of women to violence. When separated from their children, women had in order to see them, to come into contact with their violent ex-partners. Statutory services further these negative outcomes in several ways: via the courts, via the voluntary relinquishing of children and via contact and residence arrangements. Social services may access every service available for women when there is violent abuse by men of children if total support for the children is expressed by the non-abusing mother. These same services are often unable to act decisively to assist an abused woman. First, social services rarely see their role as extending beyond a referral to other agencies, although this may occasionally include being available for the woman if she calls at the office. Second, they usually limit their role to keeping a watchful eye on the children. Children witnessing violence to their mothers and living in homes characterised by repeated violence was not seen as sufficiently serious to necessitate action by social services for any of the Asian and white women in the research. Only direct attacks on children initiated child protection action, although this did not always happen and the children did not always find the responses helpful.

The norm is marginal involvement with women who are being systematically abused and their children when they are witnessing violence only. This changes with civil law proceedings for residence and contact when mediation and court reports require greater involvement. Social work-trained court welfare officers may not understand the impact of witnessing violence on children's relationships with the victimised mother nor the personal emotional crisis that this creates for her. Because violence affects emotional life, violence against women in their homes may lead to problems in relationships between mothers and children or to the disruption of relationships through the residence of children legally passing to abusing fathers. In this study, abusing fathers were able to present themselves in such a way that their violence to the mother was regarded as unimportant and non-damaging to the children. The success of abusing men in achieving positive court-mandated outcomes reflects the higher social status enjoyed by husbands and fathers in relation to wives and mothers.

Attention, if directed towards the impact of violence by men on the mother–child relationship, could develop more helpful strategies and services for mothers and children, and thereby protect children. A new look is needed at policies and professional practices that have the effect, however unintended, of continuing and facilitating contact between violent men, women and children.

Violence against workers

During the 1990s, the danger of assault began to be recognised in residential, day care and fieldwork settings, with residential care presenting the highest risk (Balloch *et al.*, 1995). Approaches include special training on how to deal with violent and paired visits to some homes. Recognising that responses to them are gendered and include the way in which gender roles are constructed is a way of beginning to rethink practice with women who are being repeatedly assaulted or abused in other ways.

The study of social and care work responses to violence against wives and co-habitees illustrates that these patterns of interpersonal behaviour are not just questions of individual personality difference, or socialisation, or the interaction between the couple, but are the expression of a system of stratification in which differential status is an emergent property of the distribution of power. Marriage relations are not just about different uses of power but about a system of heterosexual relations in which violence against wives is still socially tolerated. This is why the problems women bring that arise from fulfilling domestic and caring functions seem so intractable. It is also why women's identity and self-esteem are adversely affected when maintaining relationships and giving care become problematic.

Questions

1. Can you think of situations in which the power of men is used to control the activities of women in and out of the home:
   (i) Within the family?
   (ii) Within families using services?
2. How do the women concerned fight back?
   (i) What strategies for survival or getting their own way do the women in your family adopt?
   (ii) What strategies for survival or getting their own way do the women service users you work with adopt?
3. Think in turn of each resource available in marriage, that is, money, social status, threat and use of force, and friendship or love.
   (i) How is this managed within your own family?
   (ii) How is this managed within the families or service users you work with?

4. In what circumstances have you worked with a woman's husband or cohabitee? What did you learn from this?

5. Have you ever been attacked, threatened or fearful when working with a male service user? What did you learn from this? What support if any did you receive from colleagues?

6. Are there differences between the way in which you approach working with black and Asian women and your way of helping white women? Do any agencies you know treat black and Asian women differently from white women?

7. What do policies on non-racist practice mean in practical terms for black and other minority ethnic women?

6

Women, Personal Identity and Self-esteem

The aim of Chapter 6 is to draw policy and social demands on women together with their personal expectations. It begins with why, in thinking about identity, we need to explore the interrelationship between the demands made on women. Using the concept of women as agents, it explores the twin issues of how the social control of women is structured within relationships and how they, through struggle and action, in everyday encounters seek to create their own present and future. It explores the web of relationships in which women live, how women strive to overcome social disadvantages and how these may change over time. While women may be responding to victimisation, women also may victimise, particularly those more vulnerable than themselves. Women-centred practice acknowledges that, when personal and social expectations cannot be met, the loss of self-esteem and the negative impact on identity are inevitable and a starting point for practice.

Why explore the interrelationship between identity and the demands made on women?

In the 1980s edition of this book, we had difficulty in including women's employment as this was seen within social work as taking women away from their primary responsibilities of caring, marriage and family life. Now that individuals and families are expected to make provision for their own care, it is impossible to ignore employment as central for women, whether service users or workers. There are both labour market and governmental policy reasons for this change.

Women's employment is now essential, with both current and future economic implications as it:

- Keeps families with children out of poverty
- Includes re-entry into the labour market after having children
- Insures an adequate income in old age
- Enables women as lone women or single parents to survive financially on divorce and separation at a time when 1 in 3 marriages end in divorce.

Combining work with caring has been a working-class and a rural pattern of life for women for centuries. In the late 1990s, government policies, following on from the restructuring of the labour market, ensured its spread to the whole population of women. Now only those who are very rich can afford to be unemployed without both present and future economic implications.

Social policy changes around expectations for women have increased their responsibilities. A successful identity as a woman now includes both paid employment and the work of caring. Over the past 10 years since the first edition, some women have made considerable strides in building their confidence and achieving a positive identity. These are mainly women who have careers and who are in well-paid, full-time employment. They are more likely to be younger women (Wilkinson, 1994). These pressures are also experienced by men, but in a different way. Identity for men is most closely tied to employment and their capacity to be an economic provider and a protector of the family and those within it (Kempson, 1996). The fact that more men are struggling with their identity and self-esteem because of changes in the labour market and the implications of unemployment for their place in the family and community does not undermine the importance of promoting a positive identity and increased self-esteem for women.

The women and their struggles

As in the 1980s, women who use social service agencies still tend not to be in, or to be only marginally involved in, employment and not to have the qualifications that would secure them a career with an adequate income, although policies such as welfare to work and child care schemes in the late 1990s are attempting to reverse these trends. In addition, the life experience and expectations of women using social services, and indeed our own, are such that hard-won self-esteem and identity can suddenly be undermined. Breakdowns in relationships with men or children, sudden additional caring responsibilities or unexpected guilt because of an inability to provide care for a relative or being catapulted into financial dependence can quickly undermine what seemed to be a secure identity. We also know that physical and sexual assault can destroy, even if only temporarily, confidence and self-esteem as we struggle to overcome our feelings and fears about the security of our lives and our capacity to cope.

Commonly cited problems in working with women are a lack of self-esteem, depression and lack of confidence and motivation (Langham and Day, 1992; Smith and Nairne, 1995) Stevenson (1998) identified low self-esteem as a key factor for mothers failing to provide adequate care for their children. She also sees it as a key focus for practice in reducing and preventing child neglect. The passing years have added exhaustion to this list as more women cope with poverty and access to reduced resources. Surrounded by the problems of bringing up children and caring for adults in poverty within a context of underresourced support services, women service users can translate this experience into a view of themselves as failures. Women who are too ill, or too impaired or have learning difficulties too severe to be able to work, clean and care for men and children may feel guilty, as may those separated because of imprisonment or addiction to drugs or alcohol. They may think of themselves as failures because they cannot or do not care for others. A lack of care provided by others, through physical and sexual abuse in childhood or when an adult, can also result in damaged self-esteem and identity, which can resound throughout their lives. Many women bear this alone and keep secret the abuse they have suffered, or share it only with one person: reported abuse represents only a small proportion of cases (Wattam and Woodward, 1996).

Poor self-esteem in women is not a simple response to the negative social beliefs held by others, for example about a social class, ethnic group or disability, although it can be extremely painful and damaging to be dismissed in this way. To be treated as inferior because one is identified as belonging to a particular group of people is to deny the validity both of that group's culture and of oneself as a unique human being. However, the relationship between membership of a socially less-valued group and self-esteem is ill understood; for example, Solomon's (1976, p. 184) statement still holds when she says that 'We need greater understanding of the mechanisms whereby some black people have strong positive identification with their racial group while others perceive it as negative and having shame bearing associations'. Making the history and culture of black and minority ethnic women visible in positive ways is important in relation to personal identity. This point holds for any despised or rejected social group, for example lesbian women.

The able-bodiedness basic to the media presentation of beautiful women affects us all at times but holds particular stresses for disabled women (Campling, 1981; Morris, 1996). Women, like men, judge themselves against external standards. The dominant ideology does not wipe out dissenting views. Women are not simply the passive recipients of culture but find their own survival strategies, particularly support from peer groups, that can be self-affirming (Hemmings and Morris, 1997). Furthermore, the relationship of women to femininity is mediated through their group membership. Thus black and Jewish girls can be more achievement-orientated in school than the ideology would have us believe is appropriate for working-class girls in particular.

It is not our intention to present women as passive victims, but neither should we ignore the heroic struggles that many women endure daily. While some women have made it, others still cope in poverty and with few options open to them. We remain convinced of the conclusion made in the late 1980s by the participants on the Social Service Needs of Women courses: that there are interconnections between giving care, maintaining relationships and self-identity that are particularly problematic for women.

Recognising women as active agents

The family is the major location of the personal and social control of women. Defining women as being out of control of their families is related to what is expected of women at different times over their life cycle. Girls and young women are deemed out of control through a variety of behaviours that make their achievement of the roles of wife and mother problematic. Being sexually active is frequently cited as one problem. Once married, women are still deemed out of control through behaviours that interfere with caring for others. This can be expressed through substance abuse, shop lifting, heterosexuality or homosexuality, or through housekeeping and services to husbands and children.

In terms of self-esteem and identity, however, these ways of living and relating to others can be good. Rebellion and resistance can lead to, or be expressions of, a stronger sense of self and self-worth. Single women, for example, can have better mental health than married women, and the demands made of women through the family lead, as we have seen, to breakdown and personal disintegration, as well as lowered self-esteem and an undifferentiated self. Feminist literature is full of examples of how women have reshaped their identity, often at considerable cost to themselves. *Splitting: How Many Women Can You Fit into One Body?* (1995) is the title Fay Weldon gives to one of her novels; Maya Angelou (1984, 1986) and Alice Walker (1983) are examples of women fighting through to achieve self-affirming identities.

Being a woman has different meanings for women at different times in their lives. Women work on issues of identity and self-esteem throughout life. These are not developmental aspects, like learning to walk for example, that once realised need minimal or no further effort to maintain. The specific forms taken by the expectations of others, including society as a whole, vary, but life events can create strengths and vulnerabilities. Women negotiate their way through life. Personal integrity and identity are not static qualities. The survival behaviour of women creates and maintains a sense of self-worth that enables women to continue to meet or alter the demands made upon them.

Women's survival strategies are a focus for practice. Survival behaviour is also affected by important differences between women, such as social class, ethnic group or specific life events, for example disability, mental health problems, the death of a child or debilitating illness early in life. Women are survivors and not merely victims upon whom the world acts. In the act of survival lies a reassessment of self-worth and a reintegration of self-identity. Survival involves more than perseverance or living a life of quiet desperation; it means assertion, however unobtrusively this may be expressed. Assertion, or positive action, means taking on what has to be confronted, preferably in your time, on your grounds and around your own issue. Women take positive action every day of their lives that is more than survival in hostile conditions. Sometimes, women use survival strategies that no longer fit their circumstances, undermine their self-esteem and close down options. In these cases, workers can usefully focus on developing alternatives that are less self-damaging or restrictive. Equally, strategies can be affirmed that, although uncomfortable for others, are strengthening for the woman. While survival is a useful concept, it is no longer sufficient conceptually to explain the expression of women's agency, the dynamic qualities of struggle and action in everyday encounters.

A web of relationships

Women live in a web of relationships through which family members and others intervene in women's lives (Hanmer, 1996). In their daily lives, women are active participants who not only struggle against domination, control and coercion but use skills and strategies to confront and manage in adverse social conditions, such as poverty, a lack of community resources and discrimination. Women participate actively in the web of relationships in which their lives are located, seeking and offering support, friendship and caring. Women's most important supportive relationships are often with other women in the family and with their children.

Over time, the involvement of others, their emotional support and caring, ebb and flow. Some of the most common reasons for this are sudden unexpected life events. There is no problem when support and networks are strong or are strengthened by these events – these are not the times women bring their problems to workers. More often this occurs at the death of a person close to the woman, or at life events over which there may be some but not total personal control, such as separation from close relationships through rehousing or moving, loss of employment or through serious relationship breakdown. At such times, women can lose the support of previously close relatives or friends. When those with whom women's lives are intertwined cannot, or will not, offer sufficient emotional and practical help to enable women to continue with their usual daily life, women turn to formal social agencies. Women's apparent inability to cope should be seen in relation to changes within their social networks and contexts.

The loss or transformation of close personal ties can adversely affect not just women's ability to maintain their daily life, but also their self-esteem and sense of personal worth. The intensely negative and debilitating situations experienced by women who turn to social service agencies impact on their relationships with others and on how women seek to improve their position through their relationships. This knowledge is relevant in understanding the problems women face and how these may be overcome. Crucial relationships may span four generations if grandparents are living, three if not, and can include mother and mother-in-law, father and father-in-law, brothers and brothers-in-law, sisters and sisters-in-law, and their children. They can extend laterally to include the brothers and sisters of the mother and mother-in-law, and of the father and father-in-law, and their children, and more distant relations, including on occasions friends of these relations. The woman's family of origin and, if married or in some other relationship with a man, his family may provide not only the problem, but also the emotional and practical support that women actively seek to maintain daily life for themselves and the others for whom they are responsible.

Close relationships offer reciprocated love and a belief in the self-worth of the other. These nurturing, primary relationships sustaining women's self-esteem may be offered largely and, on occasion when social networks are very restricted, solely by their children. Children can be active agents in making it possible for women to carry on and even to redouble their efforts. The frequently heard statement from women that they are carrying on for the sake of the children obscures the reciprocity within these relationships. Children can offer companionship, love and exceptional emotional sensitivity. As we have seen in Chapter 5, children intervene to prevent violence to their mothers. Emotionally sustaining relationships are essential for adequate mental health, and social isolation may arise in a number of ways.

Women try to protect those they care for most by, if they can, a non-disclosure of how bad life is for them. This is both to avoid the loss of self-esteem that can arise from not having achieved the expected socially acceptable quality of life and to protect those whom they care about most from worry, particularly when women that think there is nothing that valued others can do about their problems. Unfortunately, adults in our society often believe that children are not affected by family problems until they are old enough to speak and do so, but even newborn babies are adversely affected by negative emotional environments. Older children may not mention what they know as they think that this will avoid causing distress to their mother. Self-imposed isolation may be overcome because the valued other breaks the silence or women, either in desperation or through professional assistance, do so.

When a woman's family of origin is resident in another country, social isolation is a major danger when her marriage breaks down. Women in this situation may have less dependable access to the routine support that most of us need from time to time. Women who are socially isolated and completely friendless are seriously deprived of the means of developing and sustaining adequate self-esteem. Gaining new relationships and developing new patterns of interaction may be the single most important action a woman on her own or with the support of a worker can take. It is a means of sustaining and developing self-worth. Feeling better about oneself is important in being able to tackle other life problems constructively.

When women are socially isolated because of rehousing or relocation, or lack sufficient income to take a bus into town or employ a babysitter for the occasional night out, building social networks requires local community resources (Wilcox, 1996). Effective practice requires more than individual responses. Supporting interagency and voluntary sector initiatives is a way forward when statutory agencies do not directly undertake community development activities. Workers can also raise within their agencies issues of gaps in community resources and, along with their work colleagues, elicit support for new initiatives. While these activities may not be part of one's formal employment contract, the role of the professional and now social policy supports contribute to the development of activities that uphold the well-being of the community and individuals living in it.

Violence and women

Although the majority of physical and sexual abuse is committed by men, women can also be perpetrators. It is important to remember that some women working in social service agencies who have caring responsibilities are themselves abusers either in their families or during carrying out their professional work. The abused person may be a child or an adult who is vulnerable because of age or disability. Accepting the fact that women are sometimes abusers is seen as a challenge to feminists but can be understood using the framework of the different dimensions of power. An abuse of power is wrong whether the person is a man or a woman. The appropriate response has to be determined by an assessment of the causes and the persistence of the abuse, combined with an understanding of gender.

Many workers who are mothers or carers will have experienced stress and exhaustion, and share these experiences with women who use services. In many cases, physical abuse is the result of a crisis for the woman that has got beyond her control. Carers and mothers in these instances often express guilt about what has happened and are frightened about their loss of control (Biggs and Phillipson, 1995; DoH, 1995b). Providing support in these instances has a good chance of a successful outcome. Where the pattern of stress-induced abuse is well established, a protection plan must recognise that the required change will be more complex, will take longer and may not be achievable within the timescale for keeping the child or older person safe.

We know much less about women for whom physical and sexual abuse is integrated into their ways of relating to people or, equally importantly, how susceptible these behaviour patterns are to change and over what period. Where the interaction of parents with their children is high in criticism and low in warmth, these patterns are hard to change and likely to have longlasting effects on the children involved. Workers can find these patterns hard to spot when there is also family poverty (Stevenson, 1998). The incidence of neglect is higher among women who are dependent on alcohol or drugs, or who have low self-esteem. Understanding the different causes of abuse and neglect, and being able to intervene appropriately, is a skilled task in which the risks to children and adults needing support have to be carefully balanced. Access to skilled multidisciplinary assessment and protection planning is essential, as is skilled professional supervision for the workers involved, because the work is both complex, and emotionally demanding and distressing.

Women who use physical violence as a means of coping in relationships are viewed as extremely deviant and are, irrespective of age, likely to be penalised accordingly (Carlen and Worrall, 1987; Griffiths, 1998). The number of homicides of wives by husbands greatly exceeds that of husbands by wives, and different factors are involved. During the 1990s, the campaigns of the Justice for Women group have led to a greater recognition by the criminal justice system of the relevance of repeated violence in the killing of men by women. Their campaigns have led to several women being released from prison, beginning with Kirinjit Aluwalia and including Emma Humphries and Sarah Thornton. Violence by women is a small but significant problem for practitioners. While relatively few women are taken before the courts on charges of interpersonal crime, when this does happen, the victim is almost always known to the woman.

Feminine characteristics

There is an older tradition of analysis of women's identity: that of specifying traits thought to pertain to being female. The stereotypical list of 'feminine' characteristics includes dependence, submission, self-denial and obsequiousness. A consequence was that women were shown to be less confident, to exhibit less mastery than men and to feel out of control (Gottlieb, 1980) The problem that this framework created for women clients was recognised by participants on the Social Service

Needs of Women courses in the late 1980s. These stereotypes have been replaced in the 1990s. Women, particularly younger, well-educated women in well-paid employment, are presented as ambitious, in control, confident and achieving; equally, this does not apply all of the time (Wilkinson, 1986). Women who use social service agencies, however, are most likely to be poor. Kempson's study (1996) of living on a low income presents a different aspect of achievement: women's expertise, demonstrated in the strategies that they adopted to reduce the impact of poverty on children, did not reduce a sense of a continuous fight to cope. At a time when shopping is often seen as a leisure activity, the women in Kempson's study hated it.

To function effectively as carers, women must limit their commitments outside the home. For example, few mothers with disabled children are in employment (Lawton, 1998), this being particularly acute when there is more than one disabled child in the family. Women must give the home priority over all other activities, in spite of the fact that, as we have seen, women contribute earnings to the family income that help to keep a substantial number out of poverty. While many women succeed against the odds, prioritising the home can mean that some women are socialised out of their skills and abilities (Gottlieb, 1980). This is particularly acute as changes in the workplace have, during the 1980s and 90s, become more rapid. 'Learned helplessness' (Seligman, 1975) and the negative self-evaluation that this involves are crucial in understanding depression in women and, more generally, how their life experiences can create a lack of confidence and an underestimation of the value of their activities and capabilities. Confidence in the ability to live alone is becoming even more relevant as single-person households grow in number, at least in part unintentionally, as one-half of the women over 65 years old are widowed and one-third of people over 75 years have no surviving children (Statham, 1996).

Woman's capacity to care is based on her subordinate position to men. Women 'become highly attuned to the dominants, able to predict their reactions of pleasure and displeasure... Here... is where the long story of "feminine intuition begins"' (Baker Miller, 1976, p. 11). This is not to argue that women have no power in relation to husbands and children, but power over children is based on inequalities that end when the child grows to adulthood. The power of the parent diminishes with the child's increasing capacity to make decisions for her or himself. The House of Lords judgement in the Gillick case over the prescribing of contraceptives to young women under 16 years old without their parents' consent is an example. Power to influence husbands is, however, of a different order.

Women's powers over men are dependent on their ability to manipulate; it is covert rather than overt (Gottlieb, 1980). The husband's position of power as a male is permanent. He may choose to give up some or all of it, but the 'equality of the "equal" marriage depends on the man's refusal to use the power society has given him' (New and David, 1985, p. 232). It is equality by grace, not by right. The differential privilege of the male in relation to the female cannot be resigned; it can only be unused as it is legitimated by society. Equality in relationships can be removed either temporarily when in a bad mood (for example, when the woman becomes unemployed and loses any economic power) or in a crisis, or permanently by a man's unilateral decision.

Even if equality remains the dominant mode for the relationship, both man and woman are aware of the 'sacrifice' that he has made in terms of power lost and power gained. Both man and woman are reminded in their day-to-day actions, as well as by social acquaintances, of their personal and social deviancy.

Gender relations

Changes in the economic and social position of women have created a crisis in gender relations and concern about the stability of the heterosexual family. One of the factors that supported male power – the economic status of the man – has changed. The earning power of the woman can reduce the economic contribution of the man to the relationship and the family, and, among a growing minority, women's earning power is greater than that of men (Wilkinson, 1994). Young women are changing their expectations of what they can expect from men in terms of economic support. This response is viewed very negatively, as is any situation of living without men or achieving independence from them. Women are seen as having been 'liberated', and the view is that it is now men and masculinity that need support (Wilkinson, 1994). This adds new dimensions to the paradox of the dependent woman on whom others are dependent, as we saw in Chapter 5. These constructs and changes impact on women's identity and relationships with men. Understanding how women as social actors negotiate pathways through them is a task for workers. The task includes those who work with men, and their behaviour and identity in their relationships with women and children, and with each other (Cavanagh and Cree, 1996).

Women, caring and personal identity

Although in the late 1990s, there are psychology texts presenting both gender and black perspectives (for example Sutton, 1994; Robinson, 1995), psychology in the 1970s was largely written and researched from the male perspective. Women are defined as deviant. Broverman *et al.* (1970) concluded that psychiatrists and clinicians saw stereotypical male characteristics as mature and stereotypical female characteristics as immature. In the 1980s, Carol Gilligan (1982) argued that we needed to hear the voice of women who defined themselves differently from men. They depicted relationships to and with others 'in the connection of future mother, present wife, adopted child, or past lover'. Success in academic work or employment was seen as jeopardising their own sense of themselves and created a sense of conflict between achievement and care. Morally responsible behaviour is nurturance, responsibility, care and not hurting (Gilligan, 1982). Many more women in the 1990s experience these conflicts daily. Claire Ungerson (1983) suggests that the capacity to care is more rooted in responsiveness, flexibility and delaying meeting or ignoring one's own needs or interests than in having power to order one's own life. Women's lives may contain these two scenarios, one at work and the other at home, with the home erupting at intervals into the more ordered world of work. In contrast, Gilligan writes, 'Although the world of the self that men describe at times includes "people" and "deep attachments", no particular person or relationship is mentioned, nor is the activity of relationship portrayed in the context of self-description... the male "I" is defined in separation' (1982, pp. 160–1). Gilligan argued that women and men are each guided by a different ideology. For women, 'attachment is supported by the ethic of care', while for men, 'separation is justified by an ethic of rights' (1982, p. 164). She concluded that women should be working towards an understanding grounded in the knowledge that 'the absolute of care, defined initially as not hurting others, becomes complicated through a recognition of the need for personal integrity' (1982, p. 166). This means that women need to claim spaces, to shift at least some responsibility for caring, but for this to happen, men too must adopt the ethic of care.

Women's identity is not synonymous with the activity of caring for other people and the neglect of ourselves and other women. Instead, caring is an aspect of identity that is prominent in living our lives as women and in the work we engage in with women in the community. Three main components make women the legitimate carers of others:

- The different values placed on the social behaviour of women and men.
- The correspondence between the skills and abilities of carers, and feminine characteristics.
- Social policy reinforcement of the sex stereotyping of the role of carer.

Social policy says women must cope

Major changes cannot take place simply through the actions of individuals, including workers. There is an assumption in social policy that women are the carers and that women must cope. 'I'll manage' is an expression that echoes throughout our childhood recollections of our mothers. The structure and level of provision are based on an assumption that most care is provided by family and friends. As we have seen, this has now been given an economic value of some £3 billion per year. The few women who leave their children are deemed lacking as a woman, irrespective of the reason. The vast majority of carers, including those looking after more than one disabled child, receive no services (Pitkeathley, 1995; Lawton, 1998). This backdrop to social policy is crucial in understanding women's experiences of being carers and workers' problems in working with women in supportive ways. These include enabling women to decide either not to care for others or to claim more space for themselves.

All the major political parties' social policies implicitly place the care of others on women. The 1960s is seen by right-wing thinkers as the period in which the advance of women's rights distorted women's relationships with men and undermined the family. Describing the 1960s, Caroline New and Miriam David (1985, p. 328) say that 'any commitment to equality through the welfare state was a commitment to social and economic equality between families, not within them'. State commitment to sexual equality was in relation to men's and women's public lives and to their status in paid employment rather than to their relationships within the privatised family. Little has changed in the intervening 10 years.

There are short- and long-term actions that workers can take. Long-term solutions depend on our involvement in forums outside social work and social care to take forward a broader conception of social welfare. This includes the implications for women and family support of social inclusion and community regeneration policies. A key task is to work across agencies to promote an infrastructure of support within local communities and with trade unions and employers to develop more practices that assist both men and women in reconciling the demands of work and family life. This spreads way beyond collaboration between health and social services as it requires implementing community-based strategies that support women through mainstream provision in education, training, housing, environment and transport. Within social and care work, the focus must remain on 'specific practical ideas and information on ways to serve particular women – ways that can be used, right now, to solve problems, change situation and improve lives' (Gottlieb, 1980, p. xii).

Social behaviour and social values

Being a wife and a mother, and giving care, are seen as more important for a woman than being a husband, a father and a carer is for men. For men, the roles of procreator, economic provider and worker are stressed. Although Wilkinson (1994) found a significant percentage of young women who did not want children and who saw no connection between feeling fulfilled and having children, these views are not always sustained throughout a woman's childbearing years. The reason for the change may be because of a reassessment of how she sees herself or because of a relationship in which having a child becomes significant. Similarly, a proportion of childless women still put themselves through difficult and stressful infertility treatment even though they are aware of the odds against their having a child. The 'oddity' of the single, childless woman is tied to her separateness from both men and children. She has no-one but herself to care for. Living with other women is still discounted as a legitimate way of caring, because whatever the reality in practice, women are not seen to be in need of being looked after except when they are very young, very old or very ill.

Caring creates cohesion between the home life of women and employment. It is a work role whose form and content is shaped, and continually reshaped, by our intimate social and sexual relationships. Women 'negotiate their entrée into these intimate relationships and into the wider structures of the community, the state and the economy which surround them' (Graham, 1984, pp. 29–30). The paid work that women are most likely to undertake involves elements of care and service, and women's entry into the labour market in large numbers has been substantially based on the growth of the service sector. Social work and social care conform to this pattern. Eighty-six per cent of the statutory agencies' workforce is women (Balloch *et al.*, 1995, 1998). The picture is similar in the private and voluntary sectors. There is also a growing number of people, many of whom are women, who are directly purchasing social care for children, adults and themselves.

Work involving care and service contains an emotional element even when the work is paid employment and part of the capitalist mode of production. Psychological distance has to be created so that the individuals for whom care and service are being provided are not seen in the same way as family, relatives, friends and neighbours. This is an aspect of training for practice that students often find confusing and distasteful. Training to create distance can have little success when there is close involvement in providing personal care. The unpaid, unofficial work undertaken by some home care workers who provide the additional support for older people in their own time is an example of how emotional ties developed through caring tasks override the limitations imposed by job descriptions and care packages based on time and cost (Sinclair *et al.*, 1990). There are many stories known to us personally where this has happened. The unpaid and unofficial activities of home care workers have enabled elderly frail people to stay at home longer than would have otherwise been possible. This is another resource: an additional contribution made by women who are the vast majority of home care workers.

Our paid work is usually fitted around what we and others agree are our responsibilities for family. An expected emotional element is the distinctive feature of the work that women undertake within the family and with relatives, friends and neighbours. The care of children and relatives may be given without love, but the expectation is that it will be present. As women, whether mothers, wives or daughters, that is what we believe and hope will happen. In this situation, psychological distance from those for whom care is provided is seen as problematic.

Abilities and skills required in caring

Clare Ungerson (1983) provides the following list of abilities and skills needed for professional caring:

- Time, with short notice availability, and in flexible amounts
- High levels of domestic skill, for example, in cooking, cleaning and washing

- High levels of social skill, for example in talking to their clients in order to assess their present and future needs
- Skills in information-gathering about other services, and an ability to manipulate other services on the behalf of the client
- The ability to act autonomously over a wide range of tasks with widely differing skill levels
- Punctuality and reliability
- The ability to operate over a long period in fairly isolated circumstances and to engage in routine and often unpleasant tasks with the very old or people with severe learning difficulties or mental distress, where there is very little measurable success or positive response from the service user.

These skills required of anyone involved in the activity of professional caring were and remain the socially expected attributes of women in Western European society, most mothers attempting to fulfil them daily through the medium of housework and child care, and are still tied to femininity. An inability to provide care, however legitimate the reason, makes many women feel 'unsexed' (Graham, 1984), guilty and vulnerable as mothers (Morris, 1996).

Caring and masculinity

In contrast, most men are likely to feel 'unmanned' if they enter too far into caring activities and are seen to do so by other men. Lorna McKee and Margaret O'Brien, in a study of fathers caring for children on their own, concluded, 'Lone fatherhood appeared to move some men away from their own sex, from what they perceived as the usual activities and concerns of 'the average man in the streets' (1983, pp. 155–6). Women remain primarily responsible for labour in the home even when both men and women work full time (Jowell *et al.*, 1991), and the percentage of men who head one-parent families remains low in spite of the increase in the number of divorces.

Masculinity, however, is not a unified concept. David Morgan (1985) argues that there are different socially approved masculinities. Factors such as social class, ethnicity and culture, and educational attainment, to name but a few, affect the detail of approved masculine behaviour, as do the situations in which certain behaviours are called for, such as warfare. This point, of course, also applies to femininity. Exploratory studies indicate that alternative patterns of gender roles in families are not as common as is sometimes thought (Dench, 1996). Using a small sample that included women and men from minority ethnic groups, Dench found that the majority of men subscribed to the traditional gender division of labour in the family. This confirms the British Social Attitudes Survey (Jowell *et al.*, 1991). Afro-Caribbean men were the most likely to subscribe to alternative patterns. However, throughout the different groups, there was a tendency for men who favoured choice about gender roles to be living alone, to be unemployed and to feel devalued by society. These factors did not apply to women in the study.

A loss of masculine identity is particularly felt when men cross over into intimate areas of care such as washing and caring for bodies and the cleaning of faeces and human dirt. These activities are core characteristics of caring identified as suitable for women. Ungerson (1983) argues that this points to a line that, if crossed, threatens men's sense of personal order and that of the people with whom they are emotionally involved. Woman have a virtual monopoly in contemporary British society in dealing with tasks such as the management of human excreta. Ungerson uses the term 'taboo' rather than 'normal' in order to convey the idea that the transgression of a system is polluting and dangerous. The impact of crossing this line on a regular and even daily basis by male workers in residential and day care work requires more research to assist men to continue with these essentially 'deviant' tasks and to examine the consequences for the service users themselves.

Women's employment and identity

Men in direct practice are crossing boundaries into areas of work socially defined as female. Women in employment whose paid work contributes more than peripherally to their identity are entering male-defined territory, yet the knot is tied between unpaid caring and women's identity. In spite of employment being the norm for women, most women's employment is part time to fit in with commitments to family responsibilities. Many still feel that there is an ethical as well as practical competition between the demands and satisfactions of employment and home. Sometimes it can be a relief to escape from the pressures of relationships and family, but the accusation of selfishness remains a weapon that can be taken out of the cupboard at unexpected and stressful moments.

Employment has both social and psychological elements for women. Workers, like users and carers, share the same complicated psychological relationship to paid employment. The hierarchy ranging from men's work at the top, to family and women's work at the lowest point (Finch, 1983) remains the pattern in spite of economic changes, the growth of dual-career families and the contribution that women's wages make to reducing the number of families living in poverty. The woman usually follows the man when his career requires geographical mobility, while the reverse occurs only infrequently. If the energies and emotional demands of the woman's paid work become too demanding, it is seen as poaching on the rightful allocation of time to men, children and dependent adults. Joanna Trollope's novel *The Rector's Wife* (1991) illustrates how these conflicts can be played out given family and social expectations.

Social and economic policies that see employment as a solution to poverty and women's dependence on benefit, social work and social care must view the employment of women in general terms as taking them away from the family, as a source of the potential personal neglect of providing care for family members and as a cost to the state that it cannot bear. Both the employment and the unemployment of women are problematic for social policy. In the 1980s, policy could not make sense of women's employment because work for women was seen as a way out of the family. Women left the house for a set number of hours and were not available to service family members during that time; thus competition with caring responsibilities arose. Women's identity was expected to arise from, and rest upon, putting their families first. In the 1990s, there is a new contradiction between women's financial independence and their continuing dependence in the family. A consequence for women is that they are increasingly likely to face contradictory demands. Women are now expected to provide financially for their families, just as men are expected to. Different models are emerging for providing family care. Primary at the moment is that economic responsibility rests with adults whether male or female, as does providing care. The contradiction is that wages, when sufficient, can give economic independence that can be used to avoid caring as well as facilitate a higher standard of living. The woman may have to choose between these outcomes. Once a woman's survival no longer depends on her husband's wage, her state of dependency is altered. Seventy-one per cent of divorces are now initiated by the woman. She depends on her employer, her own skills and qualifications, and family friendly-policies in the workplace.

These changes, for at least some women, create problems for social policy, which is based on the two-parent family, whether confirmed by marriage or not. Gender relations and the rights of men over children become an issue.

What impact does this ordering of priorities have on women's identity? Ironically, the most revealing literature is focused on women's responses to unemployment. In the 1980s, women did not necessarily classify themselves as looking for a job, whereas a man is assumed to be. 'Few people thought of themselves as actively searching because, as housewives they did not see themselves as out of work' (Chaney, 1981). This is changing with the impetus provided by social policy. Successful identity as a woman, including that of those with care responsibilities, increasingly requires the capacity to combine care with employment.

A loss of financial independence for some women has caused a 'personal crisis commensurate with that which men experience over the loss of their breadwinner status' (Coyle, 1984, p. 107). Women have to face isolation and boredom having lost their life outside the family, with the loss of a sense of financial security, personal confidence, independence, autonomy and pride. Women, like men, miss the friendship of people at work. Women, like men, derive part of their identity from paid work (Coyle, 1984; Darling, 1990). In the 1980s, these arguments were still to be won. In the 1990s, the issues are changing, although a minority of women reject work outside the family and see their identity as been tied exclusively to the family. The question to be addressed now is what options women have when undertaking caring responsibilities for children and adults. Since successful identity for women has become the ability to combine employment with caring, women will share with men greater scrutiny over decisions that require the state to provide financial support.

Expectations and reality

During the 1980s, women entered the labour market in ever greater numbers, and by the late 1990s, governmental action on welfare entitlements has meant that women in Britain are expected to be in paid employment or training for it. This is transforming both women's and others expectations of them. Women's identity now encompasses expectations about employment and caring for men and children in the family, as well as other relatives as and when required. The combined roles of employment and caring are managed in different ways at different life stages. When women have no dependent children, there is rarely a problem with maintaining independence. When women have children, the most vulnerable time runs from late pregnancy to the children's entry into school. Women are at their greatest dependency on others, whether an individual man or the state, as well as having a high level of caring work. Their vulnerability can only be changed through employment.

People who use social service agencies are likely to be women living on benefits. They also may be living with men on benefits. One in 10 families has no wage earner (Dorling, 1995). These are the women and men who are most affected by the government's current employment policies. Workers can assist by linking them or developing networks of support when these do not exist so that women and their families can be included in the mainstream.

Although there are now expectations and sanctions to ensure that women are in the labour market, the imperfect working of systems means that paid employment is not always possible. For example, women who are carers may have given up work because the level of support available was insufficient or of too low a standard, or because, having just obtained additional responsibilities for care, they could not find adequate help to maintain their employment at a point of crisis. While carers now have the right to independent assessment, the issue of resources and a proper recognition of women's rights remains. The Community Care (Carer's Recognition) Act 1995 marks a change. Provision still varies between different parts of the UK, as does the involvement of users and carers in planning and developing the provision that would make a difference in their lives. The context for this is that the carer and the person needing support are often both women, and their needs may conflict.

Extending women's identity to include paid work can greatly add to women's load. It is notable that women who achieve posts of responsibility often do not have children and may remain unmarried. This is a dramatic change in expectations over the past 60 years. Remaining unmarried was, prior to the end of the World War II, a legal requirement for women's employment in many posts, for example teaching, and a employer's requirement in other work, for example banking. Equal opportunities policies and legislation altered this and in so doing reduced the control of individual men over women through marriage. Women welcomed this greater independence, as proved by their greater voluntary entry into the labour market. However, the demands on women in marriage and family life have not shifted substantially. For workers, this means assessing women's ability to care in the context of life as a working wife, mother and/or daughter. The focus needs to be on obtaining resources for women, including expanding their support network within the community, to enable them to carry a double and even triple burden. When women expect this of themselves, an inability to undertake all this work successfully, can damage self-esteem.

Practice requires a focus on women's identity, self-image and self-esteem in a context of multiple expectations by and for women. It means tackling how women can begin to see themselves as capable of standing alone, or recognising that they have rights as well as responsibilities, and demanding resources as well as giving service. We cannot do this work with the women who use services if we do not perceive its relevance to ourselves; all of us are involved in these processes. Service users are not the only women who experience conflict over identity and low self-esteem. This can be shared with women workers and is an issue for both personal and working life. Because of this, we next explore issues surrounding gender in the workplace. We begin by looking at the conditions of employment facing women in social work and social care.

Questions

1. How many of the women you work with would you describe as depressed? How important do you think the following are to the personal identity of the women you work with:
   (i) Caring functions undertaken by them
   (ii) Living with men
   (iii) Paid employment?
2. What variations, including cultural ones, do you observe in the importance of caring, living with men and paid employment in the personal identity of the women with whom you work?
3. Do you agree that living with other women is socially discounted as a legitimate way of caring? If yes, do you think this is right?
4. How do the abilities and skills (identified by Ungerson) required for caring affect the lives of you and your colleagues?
5. Have you observed the 'feminine' characteristics of dependence, submission, self-denial and obsequiousness in the women with whom you work? Do you think that these qualities and behaviours are linked to the depression and lack of self-esteem of your service users or carers?

6. What do you think would happen if you were to focus in work with women using services on such issues as. 'Should I cope continuously?' or 'Should I be the carer?'
7. What influences prevent, and what influences promote, a positive identity for the black and minority ethnic women and disabled women with whom you work?

7

Understanding the Workplace: Men, Women and Management

Chapter 7 begins with stability and change in the work environment over the past decade. Problems with male colleagues continue to dominate and exclude women from management. The culture of the workplace that undermines women-centred practice and women workers, and how this can be countered, follows. Specific strategies are suggested.

1988–1998: What has changed?

The past decade has seen major developments in the context in which social work and social care staff are employed. Radical legislation governing work with children and families, and with adults in England and Wales, in the late 1980s and early 1990s has been followed by similar Acts in Scotland and Northern Ireland. The scope of change is greater than a mixed economy of provision and making the cost of provision a direct concern of practitioners. Major reorganisation has taken place in the NHS in hospitals and primary care, in education and in local government. The strategic planning role of the local authority puts responsibility for social concerns firmly within the corporate sphere, in which social services is but one player. The European Union's concern with the impact of social exclusion on social stability and economic development will strengthen this role and encourage its direction through the programme of grants. There have been two main emphases for practice and management: interagency and interprofessional collaboration, particularly with the NHS, and the participation of service users and carers in planning, policy-making, provision, evaluation, training and the assessment of the outcomes they want to achieve.

These developments have had an impact on the nature of teams and their membership. Teamwork has always been central to practice and management, but the understanding of who makes up a team has changed dramatically in the 10 years since the first edition of this book. Then, team members were taken to be social workers or care staff, or other professionals from the same agency. These agency-based teams exist over time even though their membership changes as staff leave or structural reorganisations take place. They are a means of organising the work, providing accountability, managing budgets and potentially providing support and staff development. The move from service-led to needs-led provision and means that the membership of teams is more appropriately defined as whoever needs to be involved to achieve the task (Smale *et al.*, 1994). These teams are often short lived. They finish when the task is completed, change when it is redefined and include people from other professions and occupational groups, service users, carers and other people in their support network. These different 'teams' are important in gendered practice because of the power issues raised. Different types of teams include:

- Workers from the same agency with the same professional background working together as an administrative and budgetary unit whose function may be as a provider or a commissioner.
- Groupings of staff with the same employer but with different fields of expertise and training based on geographical area, sometimes sharing an office base, to facilitate partnerships with local community groups, other professionals and service users and carers.
- Staff with a range of expertise brought together to provide group care, including respite care. The skills required will range from providing food, warmth and personal support and comfort, to education, skills development and therapy.
- Multidisciplinary teams working from a shared base, who have different employers and whose line management may come from a person with a different professional background in a different agency. Sometimes called 'virtual organisations', they have their own function to carry out, budgets to manage from the agencies jointly commissioning the provision, and management structure.
- User- or carer-led organisations that employ social workers and care staff. There are a growing number of examples of user and carer-led

organisations, particularly in the disability field and in minority ethnic communities. The philosophy is less one of need than of civic rights, and the manager is someone who would traditionally have been seen as 'a client'. They begin with the expertise of the people who require provision and are more likely to be talking about personal assistance than services.

- Service users directly employing personal assistants, who are paying for this either independently or under the arrangements for direct payment from the local authority. In many cases, the person employed will be a relative, but whatever the arrangement, he or she is engaged in creating a service that would traditionally have been shaped and controlled by an agency rather than the person requiring support.
- Teams in companies and industry because of the recognition that personal problems and difficulties in working relationships affect the efficient running of the company.
- Colleagues who join together as peers to share resources, such as an answering service, financial advisors and professional information, and to provide professional support to each other. A group of independent counsellors might share office resources and a reception service, and/or provide professional support for each other.
- A group of people providing a care package to a service user. For example, a team working to keep an older woman at home might include a home care worker, a community nurse, a relative who visits at weekends, meals on wheels, her doctor and a care manager. The team will intensify, decrease or cease as her circumstances change.

In the 1990s, as in the 1980s, getting support to develop woman-centred practice is a problem because gender is not an issue for many of the people in these teams.

1988–1998: What has stayed the same?

It is easy at times of rapid and interacting change and budgetary constraint for equality issues to get lost in the bustle of reorganisation and targets for cost, quantity and quality control (Ahmad, 1990). Yet understanding the complexity of teamworking, and the need to be more conscious of how gender, race and disability interact in complex ways, remains important in creating and re-creating gendered practice. There is much talk of empowerment through collaborative working, but, for many, the experience remains much the same. In both interprofessional and social and care worker-only teams, certain differences between workers exist. These are located in hierarchies of professional status, pay, training and priorities, in values or ideologies, and in the theories that underpin practice. Many understandings of the differences created through race, gender and disability, and in the production of equal opportunities policies, are superficial. There remain large differences in perception about what has been achieved through equal opportunities policies (gains in relation to race, disability and gender discrimination being, on the whole, seen as smaller by the intended beneficiaries than by white people and the non-disabled) (Lindow, 1994; People First, 1994a, b; Jones and Butt, 1995; Butt and Mirza, 1996; Morris, 1996; Butt and Box, 1997). Gendered practice means recognising both the power differentials that operate in complex ways and reaffirming the following:

- People using social services agencies are predominantly women, and those in probation predominantly men.
- A substantial proportion of the problems brought by women are gender related, that is, based around mothering, caring for dependent adults, relations with men and personal identity.
- There is covertly achieved occupational segregation at the workplace, with men grossly overrepresented in management positions, and women in the lower social work and social care grades, having lower levels of training (Balloch *et al.*, 1995, 1998)
- Men are in gender-deviant work in direct practice, particularly in residential and day care. This applies even though ideas about masculinity are changing and its diversity is becoming more accept-able. For the vast majority of men, their behaviour in terms of the amount of child and adult care they provide and their contribution to household management and domestic tasks remains low
- A fifth of women workers in social services departments had responsibilities for children, and a quarter had caring responsibilities for adults (Balloch *et al.*, 1995, 1998). Women workers share with the women who use services caring responsibilities.

In spite of significant improvements in some areas, for example sexual abuse, gender is still rarely 'picked up' or 'tuned into' as a significant dynamic in worker–worker, worker–manager or worker–service user relationships. There is no academic language, no words to describe these processes. Empathy and sensitivity are personal qualities and behaviour characteristics, not simply the act of 'picking up' or 'tuning in'. The exception is in situations in which the gender of the person using services is likely to present a sexual threat to the worker or to other users or carers, but more often than not there is silence on gender in discussions about teams and how they work.

Problems with male colleagues

We think that a competent workplace (Pottage and Evans, 1994), one that supports workers and involves service users, will recognise that gender, like race and disability, is an issue for teamwork and partnerships. In the 1980s, participants on the Social Service Needs of Women courses said that many men related to their women colleagues, including secretaries and domestic and administrative staff, in terms of gender stereotypes. This has not changed in the late 1990s. The workplace culture is still viewed by women as being masculine and unfavourable to them (Foster and Phillipson, 1994). The next questions are inevitably, if our male colleagues make us feel undermined, incompetent, overemotional and patronised:

- How do they relate to and see women using services and establish partnerships with them?
- What messages are women who use services picking up about themselves from our male colleagues?
- Are our male colleagues reinforcing learned helplessness and negative self-images in women service users and carers rather than recognising and building on strengths and sources of empowerment for women?

It is our conviction that the most likely answer to these questions, both then and now, is that women using services, as well as women workers, pick up the same messages. This is why the style of the workers and their capacity to make relationships that demonstrate respect for the person and their expertise and experience are so important (Harding and Beresford, 1996).

Imbalances in power make lower-status people more attuned to negative non-verbal messages. The vast majority of workers in social services are women. In social care, they are often providing intimate and personal assistance in people's own homes or in residential or day care centres. They are poorly paid in comparison with their social worker colleagues because the skills they bring from their experience as mothers and carers of relatives and of men are less recognised, albeit highly prized in the main by service users and carers themselves (Levin and Moriarty, 1994; Harding and Beresford, 1996). It is as well to remember that skill is an ideological construct. This low valuation of direct care skills is related to the work women do in the home. Hallet (1989) points to the irony that the washing machine engineer is regarded as skilled, whereas the worker providing personal care and assistance to enable a person to function as independently as possible is not. There are therefore imbalances in power between women workers, which have to be addressed in teamwork and through collaboration.

Communications between workers and service users are not between social equals. In direct practice, the imbalance of power between men social workers and women service users and carers is particularly marked. Being male, in and of itself, gives higher social status than being female. This, for no other reason, positions the greatest imbalance of power between men workers and women who use services. In addition, men are most likely to hold management positions (Adler *et al.*, 1993; Balloch *et al.*, 1995, 1998). The power imbalance between women workers and women using services is invariably less. Whether it is wanted or not, male workers carry a socially vested authority denied women as a sex. These gender dimensions are components of the style of the workers and of the relationships they have with people who use services. This is not to say that women never have authority over people using services, as other factors shared with their male colleagues are also important in establishing this social distance.

The dominant position of men in the agency hierarchy, including voluntary organisations' trustees and company directors (Tumin, 1993), and local authority members (Local Government Management Board, 1998), and often their race and class and the fact they are non-disabled, must be added to the power inherent in being male. All these factors make it harder for women to discount a man's sexist behaviour or attitudes. Combining gender difference with race and class increases and complicates the power relationships between workers, and worker and people using services. The complex interactions of these dimensions between workers and service users (see Chapter 2) are no less significant in worker–worker relations. These power imbalances may explain the scant reference to sexual harassment as an issue for women workers in social services organisations. The literature on sexual harassment as a problem for working women is extensive and continues to grow in spite of the development of policies and guidelines.

Understanding the history of promoting men – excluding women

The persistence of these patterns in the UK, in other parts of Europe and internationally has to be understood in order to approach changing the task strategically. It also means countering some of the myths about the role of women in the history of social work and social care.

The fact that men are in the minority working in an organisation staffed largely by women is not a disadvantage to the promotion of men. The USA National Manpower Council observed that the best way for a man to ensure his advancement is to prepare for a field of work in which the majority of the employees are women (Kadushin, 1976). This is because only men are taken seriously as competitors for management positions and there are relatively few of them for each to compete against.

There are obviously women in senior positions in the personal social services, in the professional associations and in the unions. In recent years, the number of these has been increasing, albeit from a low base. In 1987, there were 21 women directors out of 128 departments in England, Wales and Scotland. In 1997, the proportion had not changed despite an increase in the number of local authorities – there were 38 women directors out of a total of 185 departments. The proportion of women in director posts in social services/social work departments remains at about 20 per cent (Thompson and Foster, 1997). Women managers in the wider world of employment also remain the exceptions and can feel very isolated and unsupported in these positions. Apart from a temporary period following the establishment of children's departments in 1948, men have predominated in the management of social work and social care, the children's department being an exception within the welfare services in local government. The special position that women enjoyed within children's departments was short lived as these posts disappeared with the reorganisation prompted by the Seebohm Report (1968).

In the 1990s and into the next millennium, men will be managing women workers, and men will be making policies for (predominantly) women using services. Women will be responsible for carrying out these policies of monitoring and controlling the behaviour of women (Popple-stone, 1981).

The development of community work displays another pattern of the exclusion of women's influence. Women were the initiators of the new wave of community work in Britain in the 1960s, but this history has been all but lost. Community work is now defined as more of a man's than a woman's world. The women pioneers are forgotten and unacknowledged (Hanmer, 1979). As with individual and family work, the pioneers as well as the current participants in community work and local voluntary action are more likely to be women than men.

The reasons for women throughout the labour market holding few management jobs are complex. They include the persistence of the belief that the male should be and is the sole breadwinner in the family, even though this is not true in the majority of families in Britain. There is also a sense that women still carry primary responsibility for the family in a crisis or may become diverted in their attempt to maintain a balancing act between work and family responsibilities, usually at serious costs to themselves. To a large extent, this is true and will remain so unless the options available for child and adult care are greatly expanded. Women workers in the 1980s and late-1990s share these experiences with women using services. The experience of greater job insecurity has remained into the 1990s, and one of the reasons for workers moving out of social services work was redundancy through reorganisation and budget cuts (Balloch *et al.*, 1995).

There is no choice about disclosing gender. As we have seen, gender, like age, skin colour and some impairments, is visible on first contact. The assumptions about women and their hierarchy of priorities are likely to be part of the interviewing panel's hidden agenda. This remains so in the 1990s when 'to win and succeed you had to be there: at work, in the public eye' for 70–80 hours a week. (Benn, 1998). Since management often believes that commitment in both these ways is required, men are more likely to be attractive as candidates. Men are thought to be able to combine successfully both career and family. Indeed, being married is an advantage to men in the search for promotion. The opposite holds for women in social work and social care: women in senior management are still more likely to be without children and to be divorced than are men (Popplestone, 1981; Balloch *et al.*, 1995, 1998). The same applies in other occupations (Benn, 1998).

The way in which women's role in the labour market is constructed and their work patterns differ from men's means that the recruitment of women and the valuation placed on their experience still requires careful attention. For black and minority ethnic women and those with disabilities, this is all the more important, because of the complex way in which these characteristics interact with gender to discriminate further against them.

Where are we now?

This weight of history is hard to shift even though a lifetime of employment is the expectation of the vast majority of women. How long these differences will last is a matter of conjecture. Younger, highly qualified and skilled women are less likely to work part time and take breaks for family care (Wilkinson, 1994), while male working patterns are changing slowly, as is the definition of what constitutes a man's job. Nineteen ninety-five was the first year that male complaints about job discrimination on the basis of gender outnumbered those of women (EOC, 1996). As full-time jobs in industry have diminished, albeit only marginally, and jobs in service industries, of which social work and social care are parts, have increased, young men in particular are looking to areas of employment that were previously peopled by women.

Is being a woman still a disqualification?

Wilkinson's study of 18–34-year-olds sees women as the 'drivers of change' (1994, p. 10). More women are going into the professions in greater numbers, comprising, for example, 54 per cent of newly qualified solicitors. The percentage of women in corporate management and administration rose from 11 per cent in 1979 to 19 per cent 10 years later. Wilkinson goes on to argue that there has been a 'feminisation at work' in the sense that employers are valuing flexibility and dexterity, and that there has been, and will continue to be, a growth in the service sector because of industrial globalisation (1994, p. 12). For the majority of women, however, with this has come lower wages, fewer employment rights and poorer conditions of service.

The social services workforce is, contrary to popular belief, an ageing workforce, with an older age structure than that in the workforce as a whole (Balloch *et al.*, 1995, 1998). The differences between younger and older women, and between those with professional qualifications and those without them, are significant.

In common with other industries, there is a considerable level of occupational segregation at the lower levels of the social service

hierarchy. Only 4 per cent of men were home care workers in the NISW
Workforce survey (Balloch *et al.*, 1995, 1998). The majority of these
were intending to leave for other work and had moved into it from
unemployment. In the same sample, 78 per cent of social workers were
women, and, although two-thirds of the managers were women, segregation re-occurs at the higher levels in the hierarchy. Women who break the
glass ceiling are three times as likely in the sample to be divorced,
separated or widowed (Balloch *et al.*, 1995). We do not know how many
social service departments have no women senior managers, but one
estimate is that this may be as many as 30 per cent. The picture will have
changed again with local government reorganisation, but being a woman
still puts many of us at a disadvantage.

Do women exclude themselves?

An area of debate on the 1980 Social Service Needs of Women courses
was whether women should or should not apply for management posts
and what were the consequences of doing so. The argument was that if
gender is an important dimension in practice, service delivery policy and
management, women should be applying.

A number of women on these courses had made a conscious decision
not to seek promotion. In the 1990s, the NISW Workforce study found no
difference between male and female social workers in their aspiration to
move into management, although very significant gender differences
existed in home and residential care (Balloch *et al.*, 1998). In the 1980s,
women workers thought that being a manager meant losing contact with
direct practice and other women, and required the development of characteristics that they did not value: 'ruthlessness', 'making decisions which
ignored people's needs', 'cost cutting and rationing resources' and
'getting people to do more than they thought they could cope with' were
seen as negatives. The problem of additional stress on women workers is
not resolved by non-promotion. The situation has not changed significantly over the past decade. As we shall see below, this type of management culture has increased as a result of the emphasis on targets and
budgets, and because of cuts in services and staffing in order to meet the
increased demand for services within reduced resources. Complaints of
bullying by managers are found in all types of employment (TUC, 1998),
including social service agencies. In these contexts, it is hard for women-
centred practice – or indeed any good practice – to survive. The concern

about the management of practice has become so significant that effort is being made to focus on support to develop practice and on promoting a learning culture within agencies (Pottage and Evans, 1994). Supervisors are still reported to be cutting off from the pain in users' and carers' lives. The worker, unable to share with and thereby receive support from her line manager, is left on her own. In our experience, this unshared pain and a model of management that emphasises control, as opposed to the development of the worker's potential, strengths and abilities in a supportive environment, plays a major role in creating job dissatisfaction. People in high-risk, emotionally demanding work need a supportive management style. At this time, we are all participating in the application of forms of management of the personal social services that are more appropriate to the industrial financial world. However, even there, more progressive firms are concerned about their workers because it pays off economically.

In the late 1990s, we have a more detailed understanding of how women approach their career development. Surveys of younger women show that those with qualifications have often planned their own advancement and are, in the general employment market, making considerable advances into management, at least at the lower levels (Wilkinson, 1994). In the social services, the evidence is that women social and care workers, in common with many others in other fields, make their decisions in the context of other life plans, relationships and responsibilities (Foster and Hearn, 1994). There are now a number of guides that aim to assist women in reaching complex decisions about how they want to manage their work and personal life (Foster and Phillipson, 1994; Foster, 1996). It is important to provide access to mentoring and consultancy as well as programmes that address the concerns and issues facing women moving into senior positions. Many of these women in senior management felt isolated and highly visible – this being even more pronounced for black or disabled men and women – and were moving into posts at times of considerable pressure and changes in the personal social services.

Cultures in the workplace

The working environment is not neutral but gendered, and black and disabled women face double or triple jeopardies. The environment is masculine: there is both male predominance and male culture. Organisational cultures are crucial in determining the way in which men and women relate to each other and the expectations each has of the other. In their review of equality audits in UK public bodies in the early 1990s, Maddocks and Parkin (1993, pp. 29–30) make the following points:

- Women tend to be more aware than men of gender cultures at work because they know how their behaviour is restricted by them.
- Women complained as much about how they were treated by managers and the assumptions made about themselves as they did about pay and status.
- Those with the least power had little choice but to work within the culture and could resent other women who had more opportunities than they did.
- Male managers often wrongly assumed that gender bias existed only in blue collar or male-dominated trades, that discrimination and occupation segregation were a thing of the past. In contrast, they found that 'powerful gender cultures remain'.

While corporate management usually sets the tone, different departments have their own cultures so that the power relations between employees are complex. They identified the traditional cultures of the Gentleman's Club, the Locker Room and the Barrack Yard, and three newer cultures: the Gender Blind, the Smart Macho and the Pretenders.

The gender blind

In this culture, no reference is made to personal life and experience, so women's perspectives and those of black and minority ethnic groups and disabled people are also discounted. The danger for women, and assumedly black workers and disabled people in general, is that they are encouraged to become superhuman because there is no recognition of difference.

The smart macho

Characterised as a cultural pattern in the NHS, the emphasis is on extreme competitiveness and adherence to targets regardless of cost. Managers may be either men or women. It is more ruthless than the gender blind pattern, and many of the managers are often childless and highly mobile. In this culture, 'women are faced with the same choices in 1993 as they were in 1903; if you want a career you forgo other aspects of your life', because 'whingers' do not get promoted.

The pretenders

Well-developed equality programmes exist, but little is done to promote or develop women or black people in general. This culture encourages staff to focus on the small details of behaviour in order to outdo each other in their demonstration of commitment. It produces new stereotypes for women, for example assumptions about levels of participation in meetings being the same for all irrespective of individual differences, and that all women make good managers. Maddocks and Parkin (1993) see this as dangerous because individuals are seen and can see themselves as victims rather than having the power to develop themselves.

What is clear in this analysis is that women have become, and probably always were, an integral part of maintaining these cultures because there are benefits as well as deficits in the oppression of the traditional male cultures. Different valuations placed on the same behaviour of male and female managers continue. Where wanting servicing, bad temper and a lack of time for staff's personal problems may be expected in a male manager, the same in a woman is linked to her competence as opposed to her personality. Women are as important as men in making these assessments. Women are also gatekeepers to promotion. It is not only that women do not apply, but that within these organisational cultures, there is a division between those women who want a career, and those who prioritise home and whose identity is most closely tied to it and traditional norms. Part of the lack of opportunity for women comes from the woman's own 'sense of place' (Maddocks and Parkin, 1993). Developing strategies to achieve opportunities for women and for woman-centred practice becomes a priority.

One way of remedying some of the problems that flow from deeply rooted power imbalances between men and women workers is to develop strategies for the workplace. Antidotes are needed to feeling overwhelmed by our own analysis and being absorbed into a despondent powerlessness. Collective thinking is empowering. Sharing of experience, including survival tactics, is one way of learning faster than each of us can through our own individual experiences. In agencies where there are black support groups, these are valued and used by black workers

(Balloch *et al.*, 1995); such a strategy is equally important for disabled people (Hemmings and Morris, 1997). They can enhance both practice and provision through contributing their own expertise (Jones and Butt, 1995). Becoming more gender conscious facilitates identifying and sustaining changes in the workplace that will benefit women. These include learning to have no greater expectations for female than male managers. Ultimately, however, one of the changes must be a reduction in the number of men in senior management and an increase in the number of women. But how is this to be achieved?

Countering the cultures that undermine women-centred practice and women workers

The first step in countering the impact of these cultures on women workers and the inevitable impact they have on the way in which the women who use these services are treated is to identify them and understand them. These are strong, persistent and evolving, and can rarely be overcome through the activity of an individual, however strong and determined. Where the culture of the unit or the whole organisation is receptive, working for change, using alliances and planning how to cope with opposition is possible. There is strong support, including from government in the late 1990s, for learning organisations as the only means of achieving good practice. We all have to go on learning. Managers and employers have a responsibility to work with staff to create competent organisations that support the efforts of individual workers to remain competent. Where there are considerable obstacles to women-centred practice, the tactics have to be different and include working through outside organisations. User- and carer-led organisations often have the most effective levers for change. Islands of development can be established that at minimum preserve a base for future development, and these may eventually begin to connect with each other. In times of despair despair, it is important to remember that what look like small gains can have considerable significance in the lives of the people who use services and for our colleagues.

A second task is to make full use of the philosophy of partnerships with people who use services even when the relationship is based on control, as it is in child protection and mental health services. There are a growing number of handbooks or practice guides that assist the development of user-centred practice and set out clearly the experience and perspective of service users and carers. The world of practice is evolving rapidly, and education and training programmes vary in their ability and willingness to involve service users and carers, and their organisations (Beresford and Croft, 1993; Morris, 1994; Beresford and Trevillion, 1995).

Finally, we have to keep up with what is happening to women! As we have seen in Chapter 6, there are different views on the state of women's identity. These can be quite diverse, particularly where research is talking about younger women. Disabled women are at the forefront of redefining what they expect of their lives and what support they want. They are challenging the language of care and replacing it with the status of citizen, using terms such as 'personal assistance'. The debate on young carers has been redefined as a result of their intervention and has moved from one of blaming the disabled parent to a recognition that the issue at stake is appropriate and available support. Women are the majority of the very old and of those who are living alone; they are often unsupported in our communities or living in residential care. Research on what this means for the day-to-day lives of women is providing us with new clues about where our efforts should be addressed. Some of these may seem mundane, but they are no less important for that. For example, women are more likely than men to suffer from incontinence, most of which is treatable (Le Lievre, 1996). This is no time to forget that what is often called trivial or out of proportion is what the women's movement redefined as women's issues in making the personal political.

We end this chapter with 10 strategies that we hope women workers will find useful in thinking about how they keep re-creating women-centred practice, and how to stay alive in often hostile or negative situations, contributing as we do this to the next generation of women, who will in their turn, be writing books on women, social work and social care.

Strategies

1. Make sure you have support networks and recognise that they will need to change and develop with you and your own personal and professional circumstances.
2. Develop your skills and keep up to date with research and methods of working. This increasingly includes understanding organisations and interagency and interprofessional work. This is the basis that supports our practice and enables us to pull together the resources

and support needed by the women who use services.

3. Work to maintain the focus on women users' and carers' experience and expertise, and legitimise emotions, including your own. Remember that the relationship and the style of the worker are often what gives a service its quality from the perspective of the service user.

4. Plan what issues you take up, when and how; find out what support there is for you, who will oppose you and on what grounds. Do not take on more than you are able to cope with given the reactions to what you do. Time, both yours and other people's, is crucial. Unplanned martyrdom, quite apart from its impact on you and any group you are involved with, is usually not productive. Martyrs are usually lost to the cause and future action.

5. Keep up to date on what promotes women's well-being, on their support needs and on research focusing on women's lives generally. Remember to listen to women in different age groups and economic positions, to women with disabilities and to those from minority ethnic communities. There may be issues that you will share with them later if not at present.

6. Make sure that women using services are involved in all aspects of the agency's policy and practice on user participation.

7. Do not let gender issues go off the agenda in the hustle and bustle.

8. Validate gender-conscious practice and management, and support black and disabled colleagues in having their own separate support groups and in promoting more appropriate responses and provision.

9. Pay attention to your own professional development so that your skills stay relevant and you have transferable skills in a rapidly changing scene in social care.

10. Think about and plan what you want to do with your career, including moving into management. Support women who make these moves even though you may not want to and do not expect women, including yourself, to be superwomen.

Undertaking women-centred practice requires practical approaches, building on the knowledge and ways of thinking developed in the previous chapters. Ways forward are explained in Chapter 8.

Questions

1. What are the situations, if any, that give rise to a recognition of the importance of gender on your course or in your agency? Is the focus negative or positive?

2. Can you think of examples from your own practice or placements in which a denial of gender is harmful to women workers, users and carers?

3. Do the men with whom you work relate to women colleagues in terms of gender stereotypes? If there are different responses from different men, what is the most positive and what the most negative response?

4. Have you observed differences between the concerns of men and women workers? If so, how would you define these differences?

5. Have you any experience of women managers on your course or in your agency? If so, were your expectations for them different from those of men? If yes, in what ways? Is this what you found?

6. Why are so few women managers, including black and disabled women managers, in the personal social services?

7. Do you think that you will apply for promotion? If no, why not? If yes, how does being a woman, being black or being disabled affect your thinking about your prospects?

8. Have you experienced any problems with male managers? What are or were they?

8

Developing Woman-centred Practice: Women Working with Women

Chapter 8 provides ways of developing women-centred practice based on styles of thinking, principles and methods. It begins with the recognition that workers face service users with multidimensional problems. Preparing ourselves, clarifying principles, and gender-relevant methods in work with individuals, groups and communities follow. As well as direct work with service users, women-centred practice also requires workers to devise care infrastructures that support women and to contribute to the creation of women-centred services in the community. Ways of increasing resources and involving women in decision-making practice and service development and policy-making processes are equally important. The chapter concludes with a discussion on drawing up a code for feminist practice.

Responding to multidimensional problems

The full measure of the problems facing women is that the ordinary events in our lives are stressful. As well as having a personal component, the problems of women service users are also political, social and economic. As workers, we need to find ways of working with women that address the issues of woman's unequal power, status, privilege and options. We have to find ways of working with women service users that recognise the multidimensional sources of their problems. Most often, these cannot be met by an individual worker and require the expertise and resources of a team of people, only some of whom may have expertise in social work or care work. Provision also is required to address a woman's needs rather than fit her into an existing service.

Our intervention is not unproblematic. The involvement of our agencies, if not ourselves, may well escalate rather than diminish or resolve problems for women. For many women, the contact is compulsory rather than voluntary and threatens key aspects of their own lives and those of their children (Lindow, 1994; Morris, 1996; Shemmings and Platt, 1996). For black and minority ethnic women, this can include the enforced separation of family members between countries, and for disabled women, fears that they will lose their children or access to support to maintain/regain independence. All too often, women's problems, because of their inevitability, seem not just insurmountable but immovable in any meaningful way. For example, a worker in the 1980s wrote:

> How can the angry feelings and ambivalence regarding a mother's role that is expressed by many of the mothers I work with be contained? Women feel it is their natural role to be almost totally responsible for their handicapped children, and yet they are often debilitated by the sheer burden of this work. They would like more participation by their husbands. As the social worker I often struggle with my own views and feelings. I am aware that I may be pushing against the expectations of women, for I believe raising children should be a shared job. These situations are complicated by the strong emotions which arise if a woman wants to leave her partner, but feels frightened at the prospect of bringing up a handicapped child on her own.

The range of problems contained in this example includes the nature of personal relationships as well as social expectations and economic and political issues. We find that these dilemmas have changed little over the past decade. Even women who have the economic resources and qualifications to obtain employment will experience these dilemmas, although the power to purchase supplementary care will obviously bring greater relief than is available to women who must live on low incomes. Women with disabled children experience more intensely the dilemmas faced by all women with child care responsibilities. The charge of selfishness continues to be levied at women if they seek to develop their own lives and interests, even though the evidence is that where women are educated and trained and have increased income, this directly benefits their children's health and educational attainment (World Bank, 1993). We suggest that there are stages or components in moving from what seems to be a daunting, overwhelming task to more manageable ways of working, ways that enable us to begin to untangle and address the complexity of the issues facing women service users and social worker and care workers. These include:

- Preparing ourselves
- Devising principles underpinning woman-centred practice
- Making our methods more gender relevant and thus user centred
- Linking women using services with agencies focusing on women and their needs
- Increasing resources for women both personally and in neighbourhoods and local communities
- Ensuring that women are involved in the decision-making and policy-making processes of the agency, and in the evaluation of the outcomes of services for women
- Making sure that we, and our agencies, look beyond our own boundaries to analyse how the local infrastructure supporting social care is affecting women, and doing something about it whenever possible
- Having a code for non-sexist, women-centred practice.

Preparing ourselves

How can we prepare ourselves to accept the women who use services? One major way is to challenge our own vulnerabilities away from our service users and carers so that we can work with them. A major vulnerability that we need to challenge is a sense of guilt that we may have because we see ourselves as privileged in some way. This can be an illusion thrown up to protect ourselves from the knowledge of our own vulnerabilities arising out of being women in this society. Guilt can be a defence against our own sense of loss and powerlessness. Guilt can block an acknowledgement that we, too, are vulnerable in ways very similar to those of the women who use services. For instance, our vulnerabilities may arise through an acceptance of male violence, male bullying or sexual harassment at work or home through the stress of combining employment with caring for children or adults.
    Preparation includes:

- Feeling clearer about what we are doing at work
- Recognising the importance of contributing information to strategic plans and reviews on deficits and emerging issues for women and seeing this as part of our contribution to women-centred practice

- Keeping up to date on information about women and the issues that concern them, and on development in practice and provision that support women
- Being sure of our facts and research findings
- Developing our professional skills; if we want to challenge sexist practices in our agencies and in the courts, we have to be better than rather than the same as other practitioners
- Asking for space, help and support; good supervision and training are essential
- Defining where services and polices are unhelpful, exclude women or ignore their experience
- Keeping up-to-date records within the agency of resources in the area for women.

Preparing ourselves means accepting women who use services as women and not as occupants of the social roles of wife, mother, carer or adolescent young woman. Our practice flows from the acceptance of the total person. Before we are able to work with women using services in this way, however, we must accept ourselves as total people. Because woman-centred practice is intimately bound up with accepting women in a male-preferring society, it assumes that workers can move beyond seeing a woman as Adam's rib – a secondary character – to perceiving the woman client as important in and for herself.

Devising principles to underpin woman-centred practice

Feminist practice is described as a perspective rather than a technique (Marchant and Wearing, 1986; Walker, 1990; Langham and Day, 1992; Taylor and Daly, 1995; Van den Berg, 1995; Cavanagh and Cree, 1996; Worell and Remer, 1996). First and foremost, it means liking and valuing women, including ourselves. We can then acknowledge and use our own personal experience and that of other women as a resource. We can reaffirm what women know and can do. The most fundamental precept is to believe the woman, to accept her and the problem she brings. Partnerships with service users and carers are now part of good practice, but women who use services often are not seen as whole persons. When viewed as the embodiment of social roles, the fulfillers of duties to others, the service users or the carers, their individuality and uniqueness may not be seen.

To value women, to utilise their strengths and abilities as a resource, means trying to work in non-hierarchical ways. We need to create situations, however limited, in which workers and service users can share and learn from each other. This means recognising commonalties and differences, and accepting that it is the women themselves who have to find ways through to viable solutions. This principle cannot be implemented using approaches to assessment that are primarily concerned with asking questions to satisfy the information requirements of the agency. There has to be an exchange in which the woman is a partner in the interchange of information, putting her perspective and having it valued and being part of the solution (Smale *et al.*, 1994). The most useful supports are often not ourselves, although we may create and hold open the space and provide information, but other women whose circumstances have been or are similar.

Seeing women as a resource for each other and working in non-hierarchical ways means seeing the creation of all-women groups as a legitimate and valuable means of practice. The worker's gender and ethnic origin, and whether or not he or she is disabled is significant because these dimensions are the sources of inequalities in power and social valuations (Langham and Day, 1992; Dalrymple and Burke, 1995). Women workers need to spend time with women talking about issues and experiences that are important to women. This can be an enjoyable time from which workers as well as service users and carers can gain a feeling of exhilaration. It can be a time during which information is exchanged about ways of working, support systems and ways of dealing and working with men (Cavanagh and Cree, 1996). It also provides an opportunity for women to share their survival skills and strategies, and the ways they use to have fun and to relax. Women who use services are accepted as competent, as having strengths and rights.

This perspective encourages women to shed the all pervasive guilt that burdens so many and to recognise the limits of their responsibilities or that the burden is impossible for them to manage, their 'failure to cope' needing to be reframed as 'coping well' or 'coping brilliantly'. Equally, we can encourage women to expect and even demand time for themselves, to have fun and to see 'treats' as right. All too often, 'treats' are not considered at all appropriate for adult women, and are less appropriate for young women than young men. Like gold stars and 'A' grades, they are rarely given to women. But having space, for example, from children or adults needing support, or for young women to have fun, is not a 'treat'; it is a human requirement. In part, woman-centred practice means emphasising equal sharing of resources, power and responsibility, while recognising that, in our society, women are socially, and often in personal relationships, subordinate, so that power, responsibility and resources are shared unequally.

A theme of validating feelings and emotions as a legitimate means of expression and communication with others has remained constant over the years. Although there are individuals and groups of women, mainly those who are well qualified and have careers, who have a clear sense of their own autonomy and needs (Wilkinson, 1994) and who will be seen as aggressive rather than assertive, this is less likely to apply to many of the women using services. Expressing our joys, our sorrows, our frustrations, being emotional, expressing feelings, can become a devalued activity where work is seen as completing procedures. Emotion is then seen as wastefully taking up time and interfering with securing the information required. The woman who responds emotionally can be seen as having a 'deficit personality' rather than her emotional response being interpreted as a positive resource (Hudson, 1986; Cavanagh and Cree, 1996). In a partnership approach, emotion is an integral and essential part of the process.

Feminist practice also resists pathologising women's behaviour and sexuality. It recognises that women's problems may be caused by social definitions of, for example, appropriate sexual behaviour for young women rather than their personality or behaviour. Similarly, women's strategies for coping have to be seen not as requiring treatment but rather as 'forms of resistance and struggle' that are 'functional and positive means of coping with social injustices' (Hudson, 1986). This was written in the mid-1980s about adolescent girls, but we think that it still applies today and is also relevant to working with older women. Assessment and practice are too often founded on the view that women are out of control of their lives and in need of treatment. Woman-centred practice focuses on enhancing women's sense of control and coping. At the same time, it involves examining self-defeating patterns of behaviour, including how external conditions can lead some women to become self-hating, and finding less damaging strategies.

Making our methods more gender relevant

Since women-centred practice is a perspective rather than a technique or a single method, the full range of social work and social care

approaches – individual work, group work and community development – are available to workers. There have been a number of texts
written over the past 20 years that set out the changes needed in methods
to make them women centred. These are a useful resource. Obviously, an
individual worker is unlikely to be equally or even sufficiently skilled in
all these approaches. Women-centred practice, as user-centred practice,
involves drawing together whoever is necessary to accomplish the task. It
requires interagency and interprofessional approaches as part of routine
planning, practice and provision, in addition to involving women in
decision-making and policy formation. Only by putting into practice the
principles of women-centred practice will initiatives to implement
regeneration and social inclusion policies address the current and
emerging concerns of women in ways that support them.

Work with individual women

Opportunities for women to have individual therapy or counselling can
be a necessary first step. These techniques provide an opportunity to
focus on the woman entirely; it gives her time and space for herself,
perhaps for the first time for many years. She can be treated as an adult, a
total person, and helped to clarify her situation, her view of herself, what
has happened to her, her feelings and the options open to her. While some
theoretical frameworks and their practice, for example psychoanalytic
and family therapy, can be profoundly damaging to women, women
therapists are finding means of adapting therapy so that it is woman
affirming (Marchant and Wearing, 1986; Walker, 1990; Dalrymple and
Burke, 1995; Van den Berg, 1995; Worell and Remer, 1996). Many cities
in Britain have a woman's therapy centre through which women may
obtain positive help, and a growing number of counsellors use women-
centred approaches.

Because of the tendency to stereotype women and to sexualise the
behaviour and problems of young women, it is important that we check
out other people's definitions of women's behaviour. Annie Hudson
suggests that the fears and anxieties of many workers about adolescent
girls, for example that they are uncontrollable and manipulative, also act
to constrain attempts to develop different forms of practice (Hudson,
1986; Walker, 1990). These fears are shared by other professionals in
women's lives and are a powerful influence on the way in which
behaviour is described and assessed. An assessment of running away

from home or taking overdoses may focus solely on the behaviour of the young woman. She may be deemed uncontrollable even though the origins of her behaviour are in surviving sexual abuse. The category of 'slag' is easily come by, hard to shed and often a determining factor in shaping a young woman's career through the social services agencies (McRobbie and McCabe, 1981; Hudson, 1986). Being seen as an aggressive young or older woman remains a problem even though the incident may have been a response to cumulative racial or sexual harassment, or the constant patronising of a disabled woman by a non-disabled person. Checking out information and challenging definitions is important.

Women with learning difficulties experience the impact of another stereotype. In this instance, women are seen as stupid and therefore in need of protection, which in effect excludes and marginalises them (Williams, 1992). These prejudices are intensified for black women with learning difficulties. Susan Sternfeld (1993), in her research in the USA, found that through working with the women on what they had learnt 'the hard way' through the acts of daily living, the women gained greater confidence and control over their lives.

Ways of working with women should validate women's strengths. They should reinforce how women have dealt with their situations up to now and seek to build on women's coping skills. Workers need to form relationships that enable both the woman and the worker to look at how successful the woman is in problem-solving. This means adopting an approach to working that maximises the woman's capacity to contribute to the definition of the problem, enabling her to negotiate over any conflicts or differences in perspectives and to find an option that best fits her and the situation she is facing. The approach recognises that the woman may need an advocate where there are special needs and locates the worker not as the expert in the person's problems, but as someone who contributes particular skills in communication, understanding different perspectives, handling conflicts and negotiation, and has access to information and possible to provision.

Ways of working with women include:

- Relating to the service user or carer as a woman
- Assuming women's oppression and lack of choices
- Exploring choices and challenging where there appear to be none
- Validating the presence of unhappiness in many women's lives
- Recognising that some women disagree with feminist views
- Being aware that effective communication means making sure that the

approaches and the language used are those the women find most comfortable; this includes knowing that some women are non-readers and others may prefer to use pictures, songs or poems as better ways of communicating

- Finding an appropriate form of communication that enables women to describe and think through their oppression and its relevance to their circumstances and the action they decide they want to take
- Concentrating on limited tasks and achievable goals, no matter how small they are, and recognising that small changes can make major differences in women's lives, including our own.

Working with women can be difficult as well as rewarding. For example, working with a mother whose children are in public care means *really* trusting the mother rather than pretending to do so. If you cannot trust her, it means being open with her and recognising that the work you will be doing is that of monitoring and surveillance rather than counselling or support (Shemmings and Platt, 1996). The same issues arise in mental health, particularly where statutory powers are involved (Lindow, 1994). This openness and honesty is encouraged in policies and textbooks but not always within agencies, where concerns with liability can militate against it. Indeed, one of the key issues for people using services is that of reparation when things have gone wrong or been handled poorly. As for all of us, someone saying 'sorry' is important, even though it may not remove the hurt (Harding and Beresford, 1996; Shemmings and Platt, 1996; Amphlett *et al.*, 1997).

Working with women in groups

A primary method of overcoming the disparity in power between women who use services and women workers lies in working with women in groups. Power can be increased and shared through group participation:

- Through a stress on commonalties – power differences are muted
- By having more than the worker – power is diffused
- By having more than one service user or carer — power is moved from the workers to the people who use services.

Thus the opportunities to reframe traditional or official explanations are strengthened, as are the definitions of what services would be useful and what the desired outcomes of those services are (Begum and Gillespie-Sells, 1993).

Shifting the power towards people using services is essential in the move towards user-centred services, including ourselves, since we know that people in power do not give it up easily. Once we move beyond the banner cry of 'empowerment', the differences between the perceptions of the worker and the agency, and those of service users and their organisations, about how involved and how empowered they are can diverge widely (O'Neill and Statham, 1998). It is salutary to recall that, in research on the social services workforce, there was also a significant difference in the perception of black and white staff of how seriously the organisations and colleagues took racial harassment (Balloch *et al.*, 1995, 1998). This is why we have emphasised the importance of understanding both commonalities and diversities between ourselves as workers and the women who use services.

A history embedded in the ideas of paternalism has created an environment in which people who require services often have to accept services that are inflexible and inappropriate to their needs. Professionals with limited or no direct experience of requiring or receiving services have been responsible for developing a range of provision to meet the perceived needs. Begum and Gillespie-Sells (1993) draw attention to the problems that this causes for one category of service user – disabled people, including the elderly. As their work demonstrates, the past is not easy to shift, and there is always a danger that, given our power to define, our response will be 'We already do it here' rather than genuinely listening to service users (Marsh and Fisher, 1992; Harding and Beresford, 1996). Our status and the cultures of our organisation do not easily cope with people who are supposed to be 'on the other side', making suggestions and inputs (Begum and Gillespie-Sells, 1993).

The shifts in power can lead to redefinition. Groups such as Black and In Care have powerfully described their experience, which has contributed to a redefinition of the needs of black children and young people in care, including those with impairments. For most disabled children, the major defining characteristic in their lives is their disability. It is promoted to centre stage, while the needs, wishes and aspirations of the children are pushed to one side. The problem is compounded for many black and minority ethnic children. Their disability becomes the focus of attention, their needs as black and minority ethnic children being overlooked or placed on a back burner (MacDonald, 1991). For women with learning difficulties, educational and skills groups can promote opportunities for independent living and increase their confidence (Williams, 1992). The group experience is rooted in the context of action and experience, thus building on the women's strengths and creating a culture for growth within the group (Sternfeld, 1993).

Groups composed solely of women, separatist groups, must often be argued for as co-workers and management may think that sufficient changes in the power balance between men and women have taken place to make them redundant. Although this may apply to some women in some groups, this is less likely to be the case for women who use services or even most of us when we are facing difficulties relating to our gender relationships and expectations. The primary reason why all-women groups are necessary is because women have different needs and problems, and issues of race and disability interact with gender in complex ways. Also, the quality of group processes is likely to be improved. In all-women groups, the participants work more quickly on intimate interpersonal problems, and expressions of conflict are likely to be delayed until the women have begun to trust and feel safe with each other (Van den Berg, 1995).

We know some claim that the agenda has been seized by women and that the disadvantages women previously experienced are in the past (Wilkinson, 1994). Although there are occasions on which women in groups have claimed their fair share of time and the agenda has sometimes been inappropriately dominated by them, this is not our experience in general. The relative disadvantage of women remains whether considering professionals in senior management or women who use services. All that research has shown about the conduct of men in mixed groups is applicable to mixed groups of service users; that is, that men control the introduction and pursuit of topics, the use of the available time and the lack of emotional content in conversations (Spender, 1980; Grimwood and Popplestone, 1993; Cavanagh and Cree, 1996). Women are likely to defer to men in mixed settings, instead of concentrating on their own issues. Women may be totally silenced in mixed groups, so that common issues in women's lives, such a sexual abuse and male violence, are unlikely to be raised or, if they are, the discussion is unlikely to be from the woman's perspective. The deference that women show to men in mixed groups can be overcome through an all-women's group. Women need opportunities to discuss among themselves their relationships with men.

Domestic violence has become more central in social policy because it is seen as affecting the stability of the family as well as the emotional and physical health of the child (World Bank, 1993; Saunders, 1995). Cleaver and Freeman (1995) found that, in 59 per cent of the child abuse cases reviewed, there was concurrent violence against the mother. Only by seeing that the abusing man is not unique in his treatment of her, that the frustrations and depression she experiences with childrearing and supporting adults are shared by other women, and that accepting women as sexual beings is both frightening and a problem for men, is it possible to separate her individual responsibility from the political context in which she lives. In this way, the basic principle of the women's movement, that the personal is political, takes on meaning, transforming consciousness and releasing the energy needed to confront problems. The absence of men should be argued for as constructive to the group process because women need the opportunities to create different and less stereotyped roles for themselves in relation to both women and men.

In summary, separatist groups for women are positive because women can identify commonalities as well as differences in their experiences and life situations. They can share strategies and learn new ways of conceptualising their experiences and new approaches from other women. They can:

- Confront and validate their right to feel as they do
- Learn of their right for space, to talk, to put across their point of view
- Formulate the kind of services and support they need
- See women as a support network and as a source of fun and companionship
- Overcome social isolation
- Experience autonomy, take the initiative and rehearse strategies in safety.

How to facilitate group processes

Groups can be an empowering experience for women using services and workers alike. Women often begin from a position of despair, of feeling powerless. This psychic exhaustion is paralleled by physical exhaustion. Women can feel unable to effect any change, but after sharing their despair, they can also begin to share strategies, ideas and current practice, which energises everyone. Caring and supportive feelings are generated through an emphasis on commonalities, followed by the recognition of diversities. This sharing and learning from each other as well as the opportunity to inform themselves of alternative strategies is particularly important given the heavy responsibilities that women who use services often have to carry with little or no support. They may be caring for an older person with dementia as severe as that of residents in care and nursing homes (Levin and Moriarty, 1994), or keeping their children safe from an identified abuser. In 21 per cent of the cases in Cleaver and Freeman's (1995) research, the child protection plan was based on the mother being relied upon to protect the child from the abuser who was no longer living in the household.

Mobilising group resources and enabling the group to recognise what they have already achieved requires a style of leadership that is non-hierarchical and that sees the leader's role as enabling rather than expert. Problems and solutions have to be put back into the group because the problems and issues causing despair come from our own lives, from the context of our own practice. This process can produce anger because the leader is not behaving as the expert, the superwoman who has all the answers. If leaders attempt this, however, even more anger is involved because of the inevitable unrealistic nature of any so-called solutions that are offered. This anger can be directly or indirectly expressed through sullen or passive withdrawal, or by removing oneself physically as well as mentally and emotionally, from the group. The psychological effect of powerful experts is to cast group members into a powerless, incompetent workers–service user divide that does nothing to promote participation. A non-hierarchical mode of working with leaders acting as enablers is basic to adult education. It is a strategy that facilitates the empowerment of women service users as well as workers and students.

Group processes can operate in negative ways. They can stress differences between members, thereby highlighting power imbalances. Another worker can simply increase the power of the professionals at the expense of the group members. Groups can have excluded or passive, barely participating members. Too much stress on commonalities can be oppressive by making women fearful of revealing differences, uncertainties and the compromises each has had to make in her life. Relations in groups involve the same emotional give-and-take as in one-to-one practice. Negative emotions are never eliminated through repression. Repression can never be a goal of practice. The recognition of negative emotions and their acceptance and the turning around of grief, loss, anger and hatred into a determination to rethink, to replan, to change, are as much the content of group work as individual work.

Achieving this form of practice begins with acceptance of the group member that can emanate from the recognition of commonalities. As group members recognise and articulate commonalities, the recognition of differences hovers in the background. To speak of commonality raises difference as an issue, and to speak of difference questions commonality. The worker assists the group process by understanding the way in which commonality and difference interrelate. This facilitates a sensitivity to the emotional undercurrents that inevitably arise when too much conscious attention is given to either commonality or difference. Groups begin by stressing commonalities as women become acquainted with each other. Differences then stir uneasily in the background of recognised similarities, or differences may surface through a member of the group voicing difference in a way that seems antagonistic. The worker's interventions, encouraging the expression of similarities or differences, or further discussion and comments, enable group members to find pathways through the inevitable tensions that arise between the expression of commonalities and diversities. Experiencing these group processes is an essential aspect of achieving the above goals.

Working for women through the community, and community development by developing a social care infrastructure that supports women

Working for women through the community, and community development, is now necessary given the social changes in women's lives. This involves working to achieve a social care infrastructure that supports women and women-centred services in local communities and increasing resources for women. Public health policies pull together health and well-being in a broad framework of health, housing, transport, poverty and the environment. It identifies the agencies and people with whom partnerships need to be developed. Because social care needs can only be met through a multi-agency, multidisciplinary approach, the capacity to work across agencies and professional boundaries has moved from being a marginal skill to one that is central to practice and management (Statham, 1994; O'Neill and Statham, 1998).

Many of the problems faced by women cannot be resolved through direct work, whether individually, with the family or in groups. Given women's poverty and responsibilities, an adequate infrastructure that supports social care is required in local communities (Statham, 1996). This includes housing, accessible environments for people with prams and young children, and for people with mobility impairments, safe environments to live and work in, freedom from racial harassment and violence, opportunities for employment, education and training for their children and themselves, and leisure activities.

When women are poor, they need access to the means to buy nutritious but cheap food locally as they do not have access to cars or often the money to use public transport for either in-town or out-of-town shopping. Bulk buying is not an option, even if this is more economical, because a woman's income is often less than is needed to cope. Money spent on food takes up a very high proportion of income when the income is low. The resourcefulness of women in food shopping is very considerable. It is they who do the shopping around for the bargains, wait until the end of the day when prices are reduced and ensure that there is enough food to go around for the day, but no more, so that food is rationed to last the week (Kempson, 1996).

Women also need loans to cope with emergencies in order to avoid even greater risks, such as illness caused by water being turned off or fires caused by candles when the electricity is turned off. As the state is changing the balance of responsibilities for the provision of social care towards individuals and families taking a greater share, the resources available in the neighbourhood and local community become ever more significant for those who have a limited income. Charging for services is a fact of life for many people who use services. People are having to choose according to what they can afford or do without (Balloch, 1995).

Much of the infrastructure for social care lies outside the remit of most social services agencies, but community development was pioneered by social work and social care, including through social service and social work departments. This remit and these skills need to be reclaimed in working with women because both individual and family poverty are reinforced by a poverty of resources that can accessed in the local community. In recent years, this function has become marginalised within social service and social work departments, and these same departments are in danger of becoming marginalised as the role is taken on by other departments in local government (Platt, 1996). For example, the Family Service Unit's research on antipoverty strategies found that few social services were directly involved (Cohen and Whiffen, 1995). Social policy requires the local authorities to take a corporate view of community problems and the responses to them (Platt, 1996), and to collaborate closely with the health and criminal justice systems at all stages. Examples of this include community regeneration, antipoverty and community safety programmes. The names for these activities may change, but the message remains the same – going it alone is no longer a viable approach.

Ventures such as the Zero Tolerance Campaign in Edinburgh that aim to create a climate in which violence against anyone is not acceptable, food cooperatives, community banks, schemes for reducing racial harassment, and accessible and safe environments all contribute to creating a context that can support women. Skills in involving women in these community initiatives and providing information to the public about issues affecting older people or the safety of children are becoming increasingly important. Many of these approaches are to be found in voluntary organisations and in preventative work, where the importance of the infrastructure of support for social care in the community is becoming recognised.

Working to provide women with woman-centred services in the community

A second reason for being involved in community development is to provide women with alternative services and resources. Given the structure and responsibilities of statutory agencies, one of the major sources of empowerment for women who use services is to link them with agencies such as Women's Aid, Rape Crisis and Incest Survivors, and groups for disabled women and specifically for young women, on health, employment or education and training issues. A major development in recent years has been organisations that are user led. These start from a base very different from that of many social service agencies in that they are built on the culture that values shared experience and understanding. For example, Centres for Independent Living are based in local communities and controlled by disabled people themselves. It is they who define policies, shape the services and deliver them. This control over definitions and outcomes is facilitating empowerment, and can transform disabled people's lives (Campbell, 1996; Beresford and Turner, 1997).

The introduction of direct payments to disabled people who are assessed as being in need of service will provide further impetus for the reshaping of services towards the definitions of the people who use services, including women. We should see our input as a contribution to, and not as controlling, the outcomes that the women decide they want to achieve. Many workers find it difficult to accept this view of their involvement as they fail to understand how to work with people in other than authoritarian or bureaucratic ways. The challenge is to extend this pattern of working to vulnerable groups of women through providing support and advocacy through which they can identify what they want to achieve with the limited resources made available to them.

The context in which we work has an impact on and places limitations on the way in which we can work. What we have to offer can be threatening and experienced as a loss of personal power. To understand the organisational power of our agencies to intervene in people's lives is to accept that social and care work is not an unambiguous helper: our intervention can have detrimental consequences. The statutory power of the agency can make cooperative ways of working, including the development of and support for preventative measures, difficult. This may seem contradictory, but social services, as with other state agencies, for example policing, ultimately depends upon social acceptance to validate its actions.

The potentially detrimental impact of our work is recognised in some situations, for example in criminal justice when people can be pushed up the tariff system. There is no good reason for us not to be aware of other ways and situations in which our intervention can be unhelpful or of limited help to women. Uncomfortable as the realisation may be, it is an important step to take in order to develop a woman-centred practice. By clearly focusing on the women's well-being, it becomes possible to involve agencies that are able to offer empowering experiences, thereby supplementing or replacing the need for statutory involvement.

There is a difference between referring women to agencies such as social security, the health service and even welfare rights organisations, and linking them with those that take a woman's perspective as central. Referring women to agencies such as Women's Aid, Rape Crisis or Incest Survivors, however, means viewing them in a different way. Their well-being becomes paramount, and empowering experiences therefore become an important focus for practice. In this way, women can contribute their skills and experiences rather than be defined as 'a problem' or become an object of concern. Other agencies can supplement our own work by offering a form of help unavailable in our agencies.

Increasing resources for women

Resources for women of all ages are limited. Because their needs are marginalised, so too are the services provided. For example, in the

1980s, Annie Hudson argued that while there was public and political concern with the delinquency of young males and a whole range of resources to cope with this, it was generally assumed that girls' deviant behaviour would be coped with in the boundaries of the nuclear family, where 'good parents' would be able to ensure that their daughters met the normative expectations of adolescent femininity (1986, p. 2). It is probably inevitable that the longevity of women is defined as a problem in spite of the fact that the vast majority of older people do not use long-term care, and many of those who do, for only a short period of time (Harding *et al.*, 1996).

Similar statements can be made about women and their needs in all the areas meriting intervention. Finding ways of recognising, and thereby creating, a demand for resources is an important aspect of practice, as is ensuring that the gender perspective of women is included in existing provision. Individuals and groups of workers can collect evidence of sexism and of need. Channelling information does not just have to be through the management hierarchy, although there may be interested senior managers. Other agencies interested in promoting public health and well-being also have an interest. If this seems doubtful or if rejection is certain from major agencies in the locality, other allies must be found so that issue of women's needs can be raised and met.

Few of the women's committees or equal opportunity units established in many local authorities in the 1980s remain in the 1990s, but women's issues have received greater recognition as a result of these units and committees, however short lived and vilified they might have been. Elected members and agencies in the 1990s often demonstrate greater sensitivity. The potential exists for issues to become defined as relevant for the attainment of equality on the basis of gender, sexuality, race and ethnicity, class or disability. It remains possible to raise the demands and needs of women and receive validation and resources for new initiatives for women even in a time of financial stringency. Because women's equality is on the UK, European Union and international, as well as local, agenda, however marginal and poorly defined it may be, actions on behalf of women continue to be possible. For their success, these require organisation by and support from women in the community. For example, a phenomenon of the 1990s is the growth of interagency forums within local authorities to address violence against women. These are widespread and include local authority departments, national services and voluntary groups (Hague *et al.*, 1996).

Involving women in the decision-making and policy-making processes of the agency

Community and child care policies emphasise the importance of the involvement of people using services in policies, practice and service development, evaluation and inspection. The evidence is that participation is much easier to write about than to achieve in practice. Many service users still feel that their voices either are not heard or count for little in the multitude of competing claims from powerful sectors (Harding and Beresford, 1996). By the time resources are made available, the heart of the matter may seem to be lost or transformed in such a way that negates the original intentions. Alternatively, resources that constitute a major support for women can be reduced or removed altogether, thereby increasing the likelihood of women being thrown into an unmanageable crisis. This can happen if decision-makers are outsiders to the project or if the largely male decision-makers begin to redefine what is needed in ways that fundamentally alter the delivery of resources requested by women.

The recommendations of the 1990s that service users and carers should be involved in assessments is an echo of the Seebohm Report (1968). It is ironic that the community and child care reforms, intended to spur this development forward, have led to a system of assessment that focuses on rationing services through eligibility criteria. A conflict between policies that emphasise needs-led provision and at the same time cash limits has meant that assessments can focus more on proving eligibility for a service than working with a service user or carer to devise a package of care to meet their particular needs. In addition, the concentration on high need has meant that many people who need less-intensive services will receive none at all (Platt, 1996).

There are ways to intervene positively in these negative processes. Local authorities are required to produce community care and children's plans, and to consult with local voluntary and community groups as well as the private sector. This requirement provides a formal mechanism through which women's groups and interests can be expressed. The involvement of service users and lay people in inspections of provision is another route that can be used. A beginning has been made, but there is still a long way to go. Women workers can be instrumental in supporting the efforts of both local groups within their own agencies and networks by raising the issue of whose voices and perspectives have been excluded or inadequately represented. A key feature is broadening the vision of social care beyond the resources of social service agencies. When incorporated into the broader framework of health and well-being, the analysis can contribute to reducing the blocking of social inclusion of local people so that gender issues may be fully taken into account. The worker is in a privileged position because she knows in detail agency procedures and cultures. Whether the organisation is large or small, women workers can analyse what and who is likely to support change and who will block it. Their understanding of the processes and management of change contributes to ensuring that women's voices, including their own, are heard (Smale *et al.*, 1999).

In summary, more women are needed in management in order to further the involvement of girls and women who use services in monitoring, decision-making and policy formation in social services agencies. A commitment to a woman-centred approach to practice must also involve finding ways of involving women using services in agency processes. Just as we are asking service users to reject subordination in family and community life, so women workers must do the same within their agencies in order to achieve these outcomes. Until sufficient women in social and care work refuse to continue to accept as natural or unchangeable a work hierarchy in which men direct women's work with women, children and men, these ultimate outcomes will remain elusive and the principles on which they are based unrealisable ideals.

Drawing up a code for feminist practice

In the next chapter, we present a code of woman-centred practice. It was drawn up in the 1980s by women workers attending a series of courses run by authors in different parts of the UK. This code is still relevant in the 1990s and into the next century. It remains a beginning, and we hope that you, the reader, will find it helpful and thus will add to it, refining and developing woman-centred practice. We think that drawing up a code for woman-centred practice is a useful strategy in achieving the reorientation of the work of colleagues, in increasing the understanding of work with women among the public at large and the decision-makers in central and local government and agencies, and in furthering student training.

Questions

1. In creating more manageable ways of working with woman service users, what do you think are the most important points to bear in mind when:
   (i)   Preparing ourselves
   (ii) Devising principles underpinning women-centred practice
   (iii) Making our methods more gender relevant
   (iv) Linking women service users with agencies focusing on women and their needs
   (v)   Increasing resources for women
   (vi) Ensuring that women are involved in the decision-making and policy-making processes of the agency
   (vii) Drawing up a code of women-centred practice?
   How would you see these points turned into practical statements of intent?
2. Make a list now before turning to the next page.
3. Whom can you look to for support in taking your proposals forward, and who will oppose you? Is there a first step you can successfully take?
4. Turn to the Conclusion overleaf. Compare our suggestions with yours. Amend our code of practice to take account of your ideas.

Conclusion:
A Code of Practice for
Women-centred Practice

In the preceding chapters, we have explained why we think that the assumption that gender is not an issue in social work and social care is both erroneous and dangerous. New policies and practices are needed to alter the balance of power between women and men as colleagues and in professional relationships with clients. We have two suggestions that we think should be adopted as goals immediately and implemented:

1. The reduction needs to continue in the number of men in higher levels of decision-making hierarchies in social work and social care. An increase in the number of women in the higher levels of decision-making requires a systematic plan to reduce the number of male managers. It is essential that these plans are made alongside those aimed to increase the presentation of black people and disabled people at these levels. Without this, black and disabled women will still remain doubly disadvantaged. We regard the reduction in the number of men in management as being desirable in and of itself rather than simply the way in which the number of women can be increased.

    We are not making this recommendation because we think that men or women are constitutionally incapable of change, but because gender considerations are seriously disadvantaging women as service users and as workers. Overcoming institutional sexism has its parallel in overcoming racism and other divisions between people. These are consolidated by a differential access to power and experienced through social institutions. Whether the differential power is located in gender, race, disability, age, sexuality or social class, a solution cannot be located solely in those in power vowing to behave better.

2. There should be an adoption and implementation of whole-agency policies to alter, and thereby improve, relationships between men

and women colleagues in direct practice and their immediate managers. Action to make both men and women workers more gender conscious must be directed at work both with users and carers and with colleagues. Policies must include procedures for monitoring and evaluating their effectiveness so that they become more than slogans or tokens of intent.

Both these recommendations require a changed view of women and of the relative merits of men and women in social service agencies and in the family. Thus our proposals for a code of practice for woman-centred practice involve personal awareness as well as strategies and techniques for intervention.

Awareness

1. Accept ourselves and women users and carers as women and not as the occupants of the social roles of wife, mother, carer, adolescent girl or older woman.
2. Be aware that identity is crucial but that the frame of reference for our identity as women may change over time and vary between women.
3. Be aware of the pervasiveness of sexism and how sexual stereo-typing, conditioning and discrimination can affect individual women: how they see themselves, their options, behaviour and the decisions that are taken about them and us.
4. Explore your own personal attitudes and biases about women, and use your increased understanding to deal with them.
5. Be aware of institutionalised sexism in agencies and programmes, in practice, in theories and techniques.
6. Understand the links between processes, such as socialisation, and the outcome in terms of women's personal identity and gender role behaviour. Identify the changes that take place over a woman's lifetime.
7. Be aware of the nature of the survival strategies that women have developed and used. Identify the benefits and the negatives that these strategies bring to women using services and to yourself.
8. Recognise how social definitions cause women's problems. Resist pathologising women's personalities and behaviours.

9. Be aware of the complexity and often the slowness of change, and that effecting change frequently means campaigning and making alliances outside the agency and the profession.

10. Be aware that working for change for women means being better than, not the same as, our colleagues. We need to be more skilled and better informed to be seen as competent.

11. Be aware that oppressions are often put in competition with each other for scarce resources and attention. Resist making hierarchies of what are interaction oppressions.

12. Like women and enjoy working with them. Like yourself.

Practice

1. Explore the commonalities and diversities between yourself and women using services, and between women using services, when making assessments and during practice. Use your own experience.

2. Create situations in which workers, users and carers can share and learn from each other.

3. Believe the woman, accept her and the problems she brings.

4. Support and begin all-women groups for users, carers and workers that recognise diversities as well as commonalities between women.

5. Work in non-hierarchical ways whenever possible. Use collective ways of working with women using services and within the agency.

6. Enhance women's sense of control and coping by recognising women's strategies for coping as forms of resistance and struggle.

7. Encourage the sharing of experience, resources and strategies for coping.

8. Recognise that some strategies undermine us and women using services, and that as our lives change, we have to learn new ones that will work more effectively for women users and carers and ourselves.

9. Encourage women to set limits to their responsibilities and find ways, with them, of removing or relieving some of their responsibilities. Create spaces for women, even if these are small.

10. Recognise and validate the emotions expressed by women, including ourselves; they are part of our assessments, our action and our strategies rather than impediments.

11. Work with women, and the agency, in separating individual responsibility from the social and economic context in which women live.

12. The problems that women bring are multidimensional; use the full range of methods: individual, group and community work. Learn to cross boundaries and make bridges within your own agency and between agencies and professions.
13. Find out about, devise and implement women-centred approaches. This includes finding out about, devising and implementing approaches that recognise the impact of racism and disablist attitudes and behaviour and utilise an understanding of culture and sexuality.
14. Share what you have learned with other workers; make good practice visible within your own agency and, whenever possible, more widely.
15. Check out information given to you about women using services, and challenge definitions and assessments that blame the victim.
16. Find ways of working that validate women's strengths.
17. Be honest with women even when the news is bad. Overcoming secrecy is the way to promote accountability even when power cannot be totally shared.
18. Hand back control to women. Find ways to involve women in practice and service development, in decision-making and training, and in the policy-making processes of the agency.
19. Work with others to increase resources for women.
20. Refer women to agencies that can offer empowering experiences and services, thereby supplementing your work or providing women with an alternative resource. Agencies such as Women's Aid, Rape Crisis, Black Women's Groups, Incest Survivors and Lesbian Line can identify unambiguously with women's experiences and problems.
21. Think of ways that can be used to solve problems, change situations and improve the lives of women *now*, at the time when they need help.

References

Adebowale, Victor (1998) *Young Black People and Homelessness: The Lord Pitt Memorial Lecture* (in press).

Adler, Sue, Langey, Jenny and Packer, Mary (1993) *Managing Women*, Buckingham, Open University Press.

Ahmad, Bandana (1990) *Black Perspectives in Social Work*, Birmingham, Venture Press.

Ahmad-Aziz, Arshi, Froggatt, Alison and Leueng, Tim (1992) *Improving Practice with Elders: A Training Manual*, London, CCETSW.

Alzheimer's Disease Society (1994) *Home from Home: Living Alone with Dementia*, London, Alzheimer's Disease Society.

Amphlett, Sue, Katz, Ilan and Worthing, Dave (1997) *Enquiries into Child Abuse: Partnerships with Families*, Bishop's Stortford/London, PAIN/NISW/NSPCC.

Angelou, Maya (1984) *I Know Why the Cage Bird Sings*, London, Virago.

Angelou, Maya (1986) *The Heart of the Woman*, London, Virago.

Balloch, Sue (ed.) (1995) *Charging for Care*, London, National Institute for Social Work.

Balloch, Sue, Andrew, Toby, Ginn, Jay, McLean John, Pahl, Jan and Williams, Jenny (1995) *Working in the Social Services*, London, National Institute for Social Work.

Balloch, Sue, McLean, John and Fisher, Michael (1998) *Working in the Social Services: Continuity and Change*, Bristol, Polity Press.

Barclay Report (1982) *Social Workers: Their Role and Tasks*, London, Bedford Square Press.

Barker, Diana Leonard (1980) *Sex and Generation: A Study of Courtship and Weddings*, London, Tavistock.

Begum, Nasa (1996) 'Doctor, Doctor... Disabled Women's Experience of General Practitioners', in Morris, Jenny (ed.) *Encounters with Strangers: Feminism and Disability*, London, Women's Press, pp. 168–93.

Begum, Nasa and Gillespie-Sells, K. (1993) *Towards Managing User-led Services*, London, Race Equality Unit.

Bell, Colin, and Newby, Howard (1976) 'Husbands and Wives: the dynamics of the deferential dialect', in Leonard Barker, Diana and Allen, Shelia (eds) *Dependence and Exploitation in Work and Marriage*, London, Longman, pp. 152–68.

Benn, Melissa (1998) *Madonna and Child: Towards a New Politics of Motherhood*, London, Jonathan Cape.

Beresford, Peter and Croft, Suzy (1993) *Citizen Involvement: A Practical Guide for Change*, Basingstoke, Macmillan.

Beresford, Peter and Trevillion, Steve (1995) *Developing Skills for Community: A Collaborative Approach*, Aldershot, Arena.

Beresford, Peter and Turner, Michael (1997) *It's Our Welfare: Report of the Citizen's Commission on the Future of Welfare*, London, National Institute for Social Work.

Bernard, Claudia (1997) 'Black Mothers' Emotional and Behavioural Responses to the Sexual Abuse of their Children', in Kaufman Kantor, Glenda and Jasinski, Jana (eds) *Out of Darkness: Contemporary Research Perspectives on Family Violence*, London, Sage, pp. 80–9.

Biggs, Simon and Phillipson, Chris (1995) *Elder Abuse in Perspective*, Buckingham, Open University Press.

Borkowski, Margaret, Murch, Mervyn and Walker, Val (1983) *Marital Violence: The Community Reponse*, London, Tavistock.

Bradshaw, Jonathan (1996) 'Family Policy and Poverty', *Policy Studies*, **17**(2): 93–106.

Brovernman, Inge, K., Broverman, Donald, Clarkeson, Frank, Rosenkranz, Paul and Vogel, Susan (1970) 'Sex role stereotypes: a current appraisal', *Journal of Social Issues*, **28**(2): 59–78.

Brown, George and Harris, Tirrell (1978) *Social Origins of Depression: A Study of Psychiatric Disorder in Women*, London, Tavistock.

Burden, Dianne S. and Gottlieb, Naomi (eds) (1987) *The Woman Client: Human Services in a Changing World*, New York, Tavistock.

Burghes, Louis and Brown, Mark (1995) *Single Lone Mother: Problems, Prospects and Politics,* London, Family Policy Study Centre.

Butt, Jabeer (1994) *Same Service or Equal Service? The Second Report on Social Services Departments' Implementation and Monitoring of Services for Black and Ethnic Minority Community*, London, HMSO.

Butt, Jabeer and Box, Leandra (1997) *Supportive Services, Effective Strategies: The Views of Black-led Organisations and Social Care Agencies on the Future of Social Care for Black Communities*, London, REU.

Butt, Jabeer and Mirza, Kurshida (1996) *Social Care and Black Communities*, London, HMSO.

Cambell, Elaine (1985) *The Childless Marriage: An Exploratory Study of Couples Who do not Want Children*, London, Tavistock.

Cambell, Jane (1996) 'Back to a Vision of the Future: the future of long term care for disabled people', in Harding, Tessa, Meredith, Barbara and Wistow, Gerald, *Options for Long Term Care*, London, HMSO.

Campling, Jo (1981) *Images of Ourselves: Women with Disabilities*, London, Routledge & Kegan Paul.

Canadian Panel on Violence Against Women (1993) *Changing the Landscape: Ending Violence – Achieving Equality*, Ministry of Supply and Services, Canada.

Carlen, Pat and Worrall, Anne (eds) (1987) *Gender, Crime and Justice*, Milton Keynes, Open University Press.

Cavanagh, Kate and Cree, Viviene E. (1996) *Working with Men: Feminism and Social Work*, London, Routledge.

Cavet, Judith (1998) *People Don't Understand: Children, Young People and their Families Living with Hidden Disabilities,* London, National Children's Bureau.

CCETSW (Central Council for Education and Training in Social Work) (1995) *Assuring Quality in the Diploma in Social Work – 1, Rules and Requirements for the DipSW*, London, CCETSW.

Chaney, Judith (1981) *Social Neworks and Job Information: The Situation of Women who Return to Work*, Manchester, Equal Opportunities Commission/ Social Science Research Council.

Chetwyn, M., Richie, J. with Reith, L. and Homard, M. (1996) *The Cost of Care: The Impact of Charging Policy on the Lives of Disabled People*, Bristol, Polity Press.

Cleaver, Heady, and Freeman, Pam (1995) *Parental Perspectives in Cases of Suspected Child Abuse,* London, HMSO.

Cohen, Ruth and Wiffen, Jane (1995) *Family Support and Anti-Poverty Strategies*, London, Family Service Units.

Coleman, J. and Salt, J. (eds) (1996) *Ethnicity in the Census: Volume One, Demographic Characteristics of the Ethnic Minority Population*, London, HMSO.

Commission of Enquiry into the Prevention of Child Abuse (1996) *Childhood Matters*, vol. I and vol. II. London, HMSO.

Coveney, Lal, Jackson, Margaret, Jeffreys, Shelia, Kay, Leslie and Mahony, Pat (1984) *The Sexuality Papers: Male Sexuality and the Social Control of Women*, London, Women's Press.

Coyle, Angela (1984) *Redundant Women*, London, Women's Press.

Dalrymple, Jane and Burke, Beverley (1995) *Anti-Oppressive Practice: Social Care and the Law*, Buckingham, Open University Press.

Darling, Daniel (1990) *New Social Atlas of Britain*, Chichester, John Wiley.

Delphy, Christine (1984) *Close to Home: A Materialist Analysis of Women's Oppression*, London, Hutchinson.

Dench, G. (1996) *The Place of Men in Changing Family Culture*, London, Institute of Community Studies.

Department of Health (1991) *Patterns and Outcomes in Child Placement*, London, HMSO.

Department of Health (1995a) *Lessons from the Research*, London, Department of Health.

Department of Health (1995b) *SSI Practice Guidelines: 'No Longer Afraid': The Safeguarding of Older People in Domestic Settings,* London, Social Services Inspectorate.

Dilnot, Andrew (1996) 'Is the Labour Market Working?', *Royal Society of Arts Journal*, **CXLIV**(5467): 14–19.

Dobash, Rebecca E. and Dobash, Russel (1980) *Violence Against Wives: A Case Against the Patriarchy*, Shepton Mallet, Open Books.

Dominelli, Lena and McLeod, Eileen (1989) *Feminist Social Work*, London, Macmillan.

Dorling, D. (1995) *The New Social Atlas of Britain*, Chichester, John Wiley.

Dutt, Ratna and Lyn-Cooke, Suzanne (1995) '21st Anniversary of the Struggle for Equality', *Community Care*, 24 April, p. 9.

Elman, Amy (ed.) (1996) *Sexual Politics and the European Union: The New Feminist Challenge*, Oxford, Berghahn.

Equal Opportunities Commission (1996) *Annual Report*, London, Equal Opportunities Commission.

European Women's Lobby (1993) *Confronting the Fortress*, Brussels, Parliamentary Office, European Union.

Faludi, S (1992) *Backlash: The Undeclared War Against Women*, London, Chatto & Windus.

Farrington, David (1996) *Understanding and Preventing Youth Crime,* York, Joseph Rowntree Foundation.

Ferri, Elsa and Smith, Kate (1996) *Parenting in the 1990s*, London, Family Policy Studies Institute.

Figes, Kate (1994) *Because of Her Sex: The Myth of Equality for Women in Britain*, London, Macmillan.

Finch, Janet (1983) *Married to the Job: Wives' Incorporation in Men's Work*, London, Allen & Unwin.

Finch, Janet and Groves, Dulcie (eds) (1983) *A Labour of Love: Women, Work and Caring*, London, Routledge & Kegan Paul.

Ford, Janet, Quilgars, Deborah and Rugg, Julie (1998) *Creating Jobs?: The Employment Potential of Domiciliary Care*, Bristol, Polity Press.

Foster, Gayle (1996) *Getting What You Want: A Short Guide to Career Development for Senior Managers*, London, National Institute for Social Work.

Foster, Gayle and Hearn, Barbara (1994) 'In at the Deep End', *Community Care*, 10 February, pp. 26–7.

Foster, Gayle and Phillipson, Julia (1994) *Making Positive Choices: Career Development for Women in Social Careers: What Women Can Do, What Organisations Can Do*, London, National Institute for Social Work.

Frost, Nick and Stein, Mike (1989) *The Politics of Child Welfare: Inequalities, Power and Change*, Hemel Hempstead, Harvester Wheatsheaf.

Gilligan, Carol (1982) *In a Different Voice: Psychological Theory and Women's Development*, Cambridge, Mass., Harvard University Press.

Goode, William J. (1971) 'Force and Violence in the Family', *Journal of Marriage and the Family*, **33**(4): 624–36.

Gottlieb, Naomi (ed.) (1980) *Alternative Social Services for Women*, New York, Columbia University Press.

Graham, Hilary (1987) 'Women's Poverty and Caring', in Glendenning, Victoria and Groves, Dulcie (eds) *Labour of Love*, London, Routledge & Kegan Paul, pp. 13–30.

Graham, Hilary (1984) *Women, Health and the Family*, Brighton, Harvester.

Griffiths, Roy (1988) *Community Care: Agenda for Action*, London, HMSO.

Griffiths, Sue (1998) Women's Resistance to Domestic Violence and the Defence of Provocation: How Women's Responses Demonstrated Continuing Agency in the Face of Diminishing Response Choices, PhD thesis, University of Bradford.

Grimwood, Cordelia and Popplestone, Ruth (1993) *Women, Management and Care,* Basingstoke, Macmillan.

Hague, G., Malos, E. and Dear, W. (1996) *Multi-Agency Work and Domestic violence: A National Study of Inter-agency Initiatives*, Bristol, Polity Press.

Hallet, Christine (ed.) (1989) *Women and Social Service Departments*, Brighton, Harvester Wheatsheaf.

Hanmer, Jalna (1978) 'Violence and the Social Control of Women', in Littlejohn, G., Smart, B., Wakeford, J. and Yuval-Davis, N. (eds) *Power and the State*, London, Croom Helm, pp. 217–38.

Hanmer, Jalna (1979) 'Theories and Ideologies in British Community Work', *Community Development Journal*, Autumn, pp. 200–9.

Hanmer, Jalna (1995) *Policy Development and Implementation Seminars: Patterns of Agency Contacts with Women*, Research Paper No. 12, Research Centre on Violence, Abuse and Gender Relations, Leeds Metropolitan University.

Hanmer, Jalna (1996) 'Women and Violence: Commonalities and Diversities', in Fawcett, Barbara, Featherstone, Brid, Hearn, Jeff and Toft, Christine (eds) *Violence and Gender Relations: Theories and Interventions*, London, Sage pp. 7–21.

Hanmer, Jalna (1997) 'Women and Reproduction', in Richardson, Diane and Robinson, Victoria (eds) *Introducing Women's Studies: Feminist Theory and Practice*, 2nd edn, Basingstoke, Macmillan, pp. 349–74.

Hanmer, Jalna and Griffiths, Sue (1998*) 'Domestic Violence and Repeat Victimisation', Briefing Note No 1/98,* Police Research Group, Home Office.

Hanmer, Jalna and Saunders, Sheila (1993) *Women, Violence and Crime Prevention*, Aldershot, Gower.

Harding, Tessa and Beresford, Peter (1996) *The Services We Expect ...*, London, National Institute for Social Work.

Harding, Tessa, Meredith, Barbara and Wistow, Gerald (1996) *Options for Long Term Care*, London, HMSO.

Haskey, J (1991) 'Estimated Number of One Parent Families and their Prevalence in Great Britain', *Population Trends,* (78): 5–19.

Heise, L, Pitanguy and Germain, A (1994) *Violence Against Women: The Hidden Health Burden*, World Bank Discussion Paper. Oxford, Oxford University Press.

Hemmings, Susan and Morris, Jenny (1997) *Community Care and Disabled People's Rights: Training Project*, NISW Briefing, No. 22, London, National Institute for Social Work.

Hester, M. and Radford, J. (1996) *Domestic Violence and Child Contact Arrangements in England and Wales*, Bristol, Polity Press.

Hill, John M. (1977) *The Social and Psychological Impact of Unemployment*, London, Tavistock.

Hills, John (1995) *Income and Wealth*, York, Joseph Rowntree Foundation.

Holmes, C., Cooper, B., and Levy, R. (1995) 'Dementia Known to Mental Health Services: First Findings of Case Register for a Defined Elderly Population', *International Journal of Geriatric Psychiatry*, **10**(10): 875–81.

Homer, M., Leonard, A., and Taylor, P. (1984) *Private Violence: Public Shame*, Cleveland Refuge and Aid for Women and Children.

Hooks, Bell (1981) *Yearning, Race Gender and Cultural Politics*, London, Turnaround.

Hudson, Annie (1986) Troublesome Girls: Towards Alternative Definitions and Strategies, in *Girls in Trouble – Whose Problem? New Approaches to Work with Young Women for Social Work Agencies*, London, Rainer Foundation in conjunction with CCETSW and the Adolescents Project.

Jeffreys, Shelia (1985) *The Spinster and Her Enemies: Feminism and Sexuality 1880–1930*, London, Pandora Press.

Jones, Adele and Butt, Jabeer (1995) *Taking the Initiative: The Report of a National Study Assessing Service Provision to Black Children and Families*, London, NSPCC.

Joshi, Heather, Dale, Angela, Ward, Clare and Davies, Hugh (1995) *Dependence and Independence in the Finances of Women at 33*, York, Joseph Rowntree Foundation.

Jowell, Roger, Brook, Lindsay, Taylor, Bridget and Prior, Gillian (1991) *British Social Attitudes Survey*, 8th report, Dartmouth, SCPR.

Kadushin, Alfred (1976) 'Men in a Women's Profession', *Social Work*, **21**: 440–7.

Kearney, Patricia (1995) *Management and Practice: Complements or Alternatives*, NISW Noticeboard, London, National Institute for Social Work.

Keith, Lois (1996) 'Encounters with Strangers: The Public's Response to Disabled Women and How This Affects our Sense of Self', in Morris, Jenny (ed.) *Encounter with Strangers: Feminism and Disability*, London, Women's Press, pp. 69–88.

Keith, Lois and Morris, Jenny (1996) 'Easy Targets: A Disability Rights Perspective on the 'Children as Carers' Debate', in Morris, Jenny (ed.) *Encounter with Strangers*, London, Women's Press, pp. 89–116.

Kelly, L. (1998) *Surviving Sexual Violence*, Cambridge, Polity Press.

Kempson, Elaine (1996) *Life on a Low Income*, York, Joseph Rowntree Foundation.

Klein, Renate (1989) *Women Speak Out about their Experiences of Reproductive Medicine*, London, Pandora Press.

Langam, Mary and Day, Lesley (1992) *Women, Oppression and Social Work*, London, Routledge.

Lawton, Dot (1998) *Complex Numbers: Families with More than One Disabled Child,* York, Social Policy Research Unit.

Le Lievre, Sarah (1996) Speaking Notes on Incontinence, from a workshop in London, London, Social Services Inspectorate, Department of Health .

Levin, Enid and Moriarty, Jo (1994) *Better for the Break*, London, HMSO.

Lindow, Viv (1994) *Self Help and Alternatives*, London, Mental Health Foundation.

Local Government Associations (1995) *Towards a New Consensus*, London, Association of District Councils, Association of County Councils, Association of Metropolitan Authorities.

Lorde, Audre (1981) 'An Open Letter to Mary Daly', in Moraga, Cherie and Anzaldua, Gloria (eds) *This Bridge Called My Back: Writings of Radical Women of Color*, New York, Kitchen Table Press.

Lorde, Audre (1984) *Sister Outsider*, Trumansburg, NY, Crossing Press.

Low Income Project Team for the Nutrition Task Force (1996) *Low Income, Nutrition and Health: Strategies for Improvement*, Health of the Nation, London, Department of Health.

MacDonald, Shelia (1991) *All Equal Under the Act?* London, Race Equality Unit.

McKee, Lorna and O'Brien, Margaret (eds) (1983) 'Taking Gender Seriously', in Gamarinkow, Eva, Morgan, David, Purvis, June and Taylorson, Daphne, *The Public and the Private*, London, Heinemann, pp. 146–61.

McRobbie, Angela and McCabe, Trisha (eds) (1981) *Feminism for Girls: An Adventure Story*, London, Routledge & Kegan Paul.

Maddock, Su, and Parkin, Di (1993) 'Gender Cultures: How They Affect Men and Women at Work', *Women and Management Review*, **8**(2): 70–84.

Marchant, Helen and Wearing, Betsy (eds) (1986) *Gender Reclaimed: Women in Social Work*, Marickville, New Zealand, Hale & Leimonger.

Marsh, Peter and Fisher, Michael (1992) *Good Intentions: Developing Partnerships in Social Services*, York, Joseph Rowntree Foundation.

Mayhew, Pat, Maung, Natalie Aye and Mirrless-Black, Catriona (1993) *The 1992 British Crime Survey*, Home Office Research Study No. 132, London, HMSO.

Maynard, Mary (1985) 'The Response of Social Workers to Domestic Violence', in Pahl, Jan (ed.) *Private Violence and Public Policy: The Needs of Battered Women and the Response of the Public Services,* London, Routledge & Kegan Paul, pp. 125–41.

Miller, Jean Baker (1976) *Towards a New Psychology of Women*, Harmondsworth, Penguin.

Mooney, Jayne (1993) *The Hidden Figure: Domestic Violence in North London*, Islington Council, Police and Crime Prevention Unit.

Moraga, Cherrie and Anzaldua, Gloria (eds) (1981) *This Bridge Called My Back: Writings of Radical Women of Color*, New York, Kitchen Table Press.

Morgan, David (1985) *The Family, Politics and Social Theory*, London, Routledge & Kegan Paul.

Morris, Jenny (1993a) *Independent Lives? Community Care and Disabled People*, London, Macmillan.

Morris, Jenny (1993b) *Disabled Lives: Many Voices, One Message*, York, Joseph Rowntree Foundation.

Morris, Jenny (1994) *The Shape of Things to Come: User-led Social Services*, London, National Institute for Social Work.

Morris, Jenny (1995) 'Creating a Space for Absent Voices: Disabled Women's Experiences of Receiving Assistance with Daily Living Activities', *Feminist Review* (51): 68–93.

Morris, Jenny (1996) *Encounters with Strangers: Feminism and Disability*, London, Women's Press.

Mullender, Audrey (1996) *Rethinking Domestic Violence: The Social Work and Probation Response*, London, Routledge.

Mullender, Audrey and Morley, Rebecca (1994) *Children Living with Domestic Violence: Putting Men's Abuse of Women on the Child Care Agenda*, London, Whiting & Birch.

National Commission of Inquiry into the Prevention of Child Abuse (1996) *Childhood Matters: Report of the National Commission of Inquiry into the Prevention of Child Abuse,* Vol. 1 & 2, London, Stationery Office.

Nelson, Sarah (1987) *Incest: Fact and Myth*, Edinburgh, Stramullion.

New, Caroline and David, Miriam (1985) *For the Sake of the Children: Making Child Care more than Women's Business*, Harmondsworth, Penguin.

Office for National Statistics (1992) *Living in Britain: Results from the 1992 General Household Survey*, London, UK Government, Office for National Statistics, Social Survey Division.

Office of Population Censuses and Surveys (1992) London, HMSO.

Office of Population Censuses and Surveys Monitor (1994) National Population Projections 1992, 94/1 January, cited in *Third Report from the Social Security Select Committee, House of Commons.*

Office of Population Censuses and Surveys (1996) *Ethnicity in the 1991 Census,* London, HMSO.

Oliver, Michael (1983) *Social Work with Disabled People*, London, Macmillan.

O'Neil, Alex and Statham, Daphne (eds) (1998) *Shaping Futures – Rights, Welfare and the Personal Social Services*, London, National Institute for Social Work.

Pahl, Jan (1989) *Money and Marriage*, Basingstoke, Macmillan.

Painter, Kate (1991) *Wife Rape, Marriage and the Law*, Faculty of Economic and Social Studies, University of Manchester.

Parker, Roy (1981) 'Tending and Social Policy', in Goldberg, E. Matilda and Hatch, Stephen (eds) *A New Look at the Personal Social Services*, Discussion Paper No. 4, London, Policy Studies Institute.

Parker, Roy, (1995) 'Child Protection Research into Practice', in *Seiff Foundation Report of Conference Proceedings: Messages from the Research*, London, Seiff.

People First (1994a) *Helping You Get the Services You Want: A Guide for People with Learning Difficulties To Help them Through the Assessment and Get the Services they Want*, London, People First/Camden Social Services.

People First (1994b) *Oi! Its my First Assessment: Everything You Ever Wanted To Know About Community Care but Nobody Bothered To Tell You*, London, People First.

People First (1994c) *Outside but not Inside yet: Leaving Hospital and Living in the Community: An Evaluation by People with Learning Disabilities*, London, People First.

Phillipson, Julia (1992) *Practising Equality: Women, Men and Social Work*, London, Central Council for Education and Social Work.

Pitkeathley, Jill (1995) 'Who Does Care', *Journal of the Royal Society of Arts*, December: 46–50.

Platt, Denise (1996) D*eveloping Eligibility Criteria for Continuing Care*, Seminar for Capita, London.

Popplestone, Ruth (1981) A Woman's Profession, unpublished paper.

Pottage, Dave and Evans, Mike (1994) *The Competent Workplace: The View from Within*, London, National Institute for Social Work.

Power House (1996) 'Power in the House: Women with Learning Difficulties Organising against Abuse', in Morris, Jenny, *Encounter with Strangers: Feminism and Disability*, London, Women's Press, pp. 135–42.

Rich, Adrienne, (1977) *Of Woman Born: Motherhood as Experience and Institution*, London, Virago.

Rich, Adrienne (1980) Compulsory Heterosexuality and Lesbian Existence, *Signs*, **5**(4): 631–60.

Richards, Margaret (1987) *Developing the Content of Practice Teaching*, Social Work Education, **6**(2): 4–9.

Rights of Women Lesbian Custody Group (1986) *Lesbian Mother's Legal Handbook*, London, Women's Press.

Robinson, Lena (1995) *Psychology for Social Workers: Black Perspectives*, London, Routledge.

Rodgers, Brian and Pryor, Jan (1998) *Divorce and Separation: The Outcomes for Children*, York, Joseph Rowntree Foundation.

Rogers, W. Stainton and Rogers, R. Stainton (1996) *Young People's Aspirations in a Changing Europe*, Hemel Hempstead, Harvester Wheatsheaf.

Rutter, Michael, (1981) *Maternal Deprivation Reassessed*, Harmondsworth, Penguin.

Saunders, Alex (1995) *It Hurts me too*, London, National Institute for Social Work, Child Line and Women's Aid.

Schneider, Justine, Knapp, Martin, Kavanagh, Shane, Beecham, Jenni and Nettan, Ann (1993) 'Elderly People with an Advanced Impairment in England: Resource Use and Costs', *Aging Society*, **13**(1): 27–50.

Schneider, Justine, Mann, Anthony, Blizard, Bob *et al.* (1997) 'Exploring Quality in Residential Care for Elderly People', *Care: The Journal of Practice and Development*, **6**(1): 7–20.

Seebohm Report (1968) *Report of the Committee on Local Authority and Allied Personal Social Services*, Cmnd 3703, London, HMSO.

Seligman, Martin (1975) *Helplessness: On Depression, Development and Death*, San Francisco, Freeman.

Shemmings, David and Platt, Dendy (1996) *Making Enquiries into Alleged Child Abuse and Neglect: Partnership with Family*, Chichester, John Wiley.

Sinclair, Ian, Parker, Roy, Leat, Diane and Williams, Jenny (1990) *Kaleidoscope of Care: A Review of the Research on Welfare Provision for Elderly People*, London, HMSO/National Institute for Social Work.

Smale, Gerry (1996) *Mapping Change and Innovation*, London, HMSO.

Smale, Gerry, Tuson, Graham, Ahmad, Bandana, Darvill, Giles, Domoney, Lynette and Sainsbury, Eric (1994) *Negotiating Care in the Community*, London, HMSO.

Smale, Gerry, Tuson, Graham and Statham, Daphne (1999) *Community Based Practice: Reinventing Social Work*, Basingstoke, Macmillan (in press).

Smith, Barbara and Smith, Beverly (1981) 'Across the Kitchen Table: Sister to Sister Dialogue', in Moraga, Cherrie and Anzaldua, Gloria (eds) *This Bridge Called my Back: Writings of Radical Women of Color*, New York, Kitchen Table Press, pp. 113–27.

Smith, Gerrilyn and Nairne, Kathy (1995) *Dealing with Depression*, 2nd edition, London, Women's Press.

S/NVQs (1997) Care Sector Consortium/Scottish Council for Vocational Qualifications, London and Edinburgh.

Social Services Inspectorate (1995) *Chief Inspector's Report*, London, Department of Health.

Social Trends (1998) Central Statistics Office, London, HMSO.

Solomon, Barbara Bryant (1976) *Black Empowerment: Social Work with Oppressed Communities*, New York, Columbia University Press.

Spender, Dale (1980) *Man Made Language*, London, Routledge & Kegan Paul.

Stark, Evan, Flitcraft, Anne and Frazier, W (1996) *Women at Risk: Domestic Violence and Women's Health*, London, Sage.

Statham, Daphne (1996) *The Future of Personal and Social Care: The Role of Social Service Organisations in the Public, Private and Voluntary Sectors*, London, National Institute for Social Work.

Sternfeld, Susan (1993) Learning the Hard Way: Women Labelled with Mental Retardation Describe their Way of Knowing, Doctoral thesis, Boston University, Mass.

Stevenson, Olive (1998) *Child Neglect, Issues and Dilemmas*, Oxford, Blackwell.

Sutton, Carol (1994) *Social Work, Community Work and Psychology*, Leicester, British Psychological Association.

Taylor, Patricia and Daly, Catherine (eds) (1995) *Gender Dilemmas in Social Work: Issues Affecting Women in the Profession*, Toronto, Canadian Scholars' Press.

Thompson, Audrey and Foster, Joy (1997) 'A Woman's Liberation', *Community Care*, 4–10 December, pp. 18–19.

Townsend, Peter (1979) *Poverty in the UK*, Harmondsworth, Penguin.

Trades Union Council (1998) *Report on Use of Help-line on Stress*, London, Trades Union Council.

Trollope, Joanna (1991) *The Rector's Wife*, London, Black Swan.

Tumin, Winifred (1993) *On Trust: Increasing the Effectiveness of Charity Trustees and Management Committees; Report of the NCVO/Charity Commission Working Party on Trustee Training*, London, National Council for Voluntary Organisations.

Ungerson, Clare (1983) 'Women and Caring: Skills, Tasks and Taboos', in Garaminkow, Eva, Morgan, David, Purvis, June and Taylorson, Daphne (eds) *The Public and the Private*, London, Heinemann, pp. 62–77.

Ungerson, Clare (ed.) (1985) *Women and Social Policy: A Reader*, London, Macmillan.

United Nations Office at the Vienna Centre for Social Development and Humanitarian Affairs (1993) *Strategies for Confronting Domestic Violence: A Resource Manual*, Vienna, United Nations.

Utting, David (1995) *Family and Parenthood: Supporting Families, Preventing Breakdown*, York, Joseph Rowntree Foundation.

Van den Berg, Nan (ed.) (1995) *Feminist Practice in the 21st Century*, Washington, National Association of Social Workers.

Vernon, Ayesha (1996) 'A Stranger in Many Camps: The Experience of Disabled Black and Ethnic Minority Women', in Morris, Jenny, *Encounter with Strangers: Feminism and Disability*, London, Women's Press, pp. 48–68.

Walker, Alice (1983) *The Color Purple*, London, Women's Press.

Walker, Alice (1984) *In Search of Our Mother's Gardens*, London, Women's Press.

Walker, Moira (1990) *Women in Therapy and Counselling*, Buckingham, Open University Press.

Wattam, Corinne and Woodward, Clare (1996) *'And Do I Abuse My Children ... No!'*, Report of the National Commission of Inquiry into the Prevention of Child Abuse, Childhood Matters, vol. 2, London, Stationery Office, pp. 43–148.

Weldon, Fay (1995) *Splitting: How Many Women Can you Fit into one Body*, London, Flamingo.

Wilcox, Paula (1996) Social Support and Women Leaving Violent Relationships: An Exploratory Longitudinal Study on a Housing Estate in Sheffield (England) of the Factors Influencing Women's Experiences of Social Support, PhD, University of Bradford.

Wilkinson, Helen (1994) *No Turning Back: Generations and Gender Quake*, London, Demos.

Wilkinson, Helen and Mulgan, Geoff (1995) *Freedom's Children: Work, Relationships and Politics for 18–34 year olds in Britain Today*, London, Demos.

Wilkinson, Sue (ed.) (1986) *Feminist Psychology: Developing Theory and Practice*, Milton Keynes, Open University Press.

Williams, Fiona (1992) 'Women with Learning Difficulties', in Langam, Mary and Day, Lesley, *Women, Oppression and Social Work*, London, Routledge, pp. 149–68.

World Bank (1993) *World Development Report: Investing in Health*, Oxford, Oxford University Press.

Worell, Judith and Remer, Pam (1996) *Feminist Perspectives in Therapy*, Chichester, John Wiley.

Index